W9-CPL-409

THE HOW AND WHY WONDER BOOK OF
OCEANOGRAPHY

Written by ROBERT SCHARFF
Illustrated by ROBERT DOREMUS
Editorial Production: DONALD D. WOLF

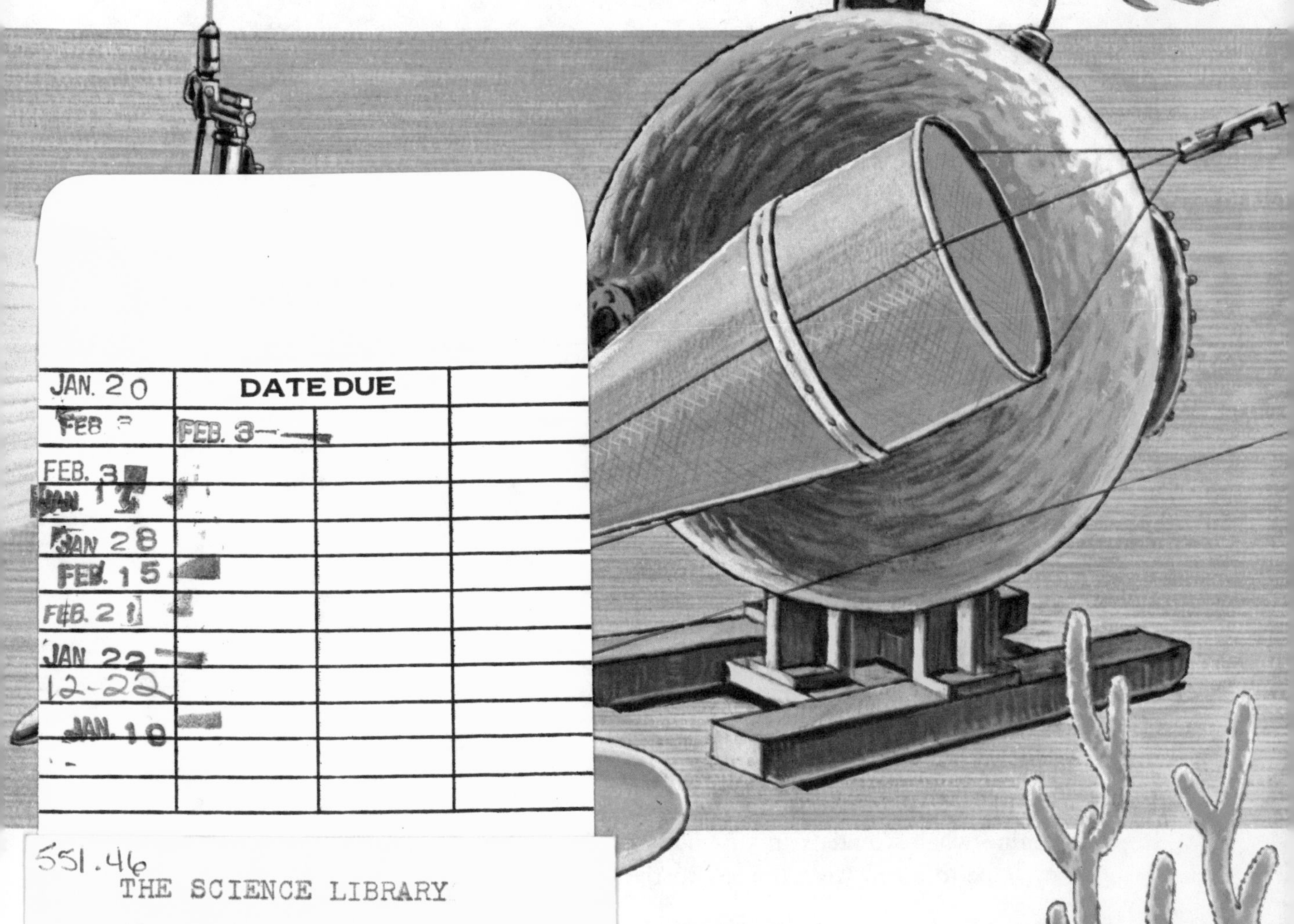

JAN. 20	DATE DUE	
FEB ?	FEB. 3	
FEB. 3		
JAN. 17		
JAN 28		
FEB. 15		
FEB. 2		
JAN 22		
12-22		
JAN. 10		

551.46
THE SCIENCE LIBRARY
VOLUME 4

...hington, D. C.

...hildren's Museum, Brooklyn, New York

Publishers • NEW YORK

WATERLOO LOCAL SCHOOL
Middle School Library Title II

Introduction

The vast expanses and the impenetrable depths of the ocean have given it a mystery that has always captured the imagination. What is mysterious about space beyond the eyes' span and distance out of arms' reach? Is it the element of danger, the fascination of the unknown, or the ever-elusive horizon? The enigma of the ocean eludes a simple explanation.

With the rapidly growing science of oceanography, however, the seas are gradually revealing their secrets. Much of the new — as well as the old — knowledge about the ocean is presented in this *How and Why Wonder Book of Oceanography*.

There is a good deal more to be fathomed — more about the directions of ocean currents and their effect on weather; the plant and animal life at different depths; the kinds and amounts of minerals in sea water; the evidence of prehistoric life; the mountains on the ocean floor. An armchair oceanographer can think of hundreds of questions. Fortunately, real oceanographers are asking such questions, too. And because each time one question about the ocean is answered, two new ones pop up, the future is exciting for oceanographers.

The *How and Why Wonder Book of Oceanography* helps readers examine what scientists in this field have already accomplished and what they hope to glean from the sea in the future.

Paul E. Blackwood

Dr. Blackwood is a professional employee in the U. S. Office of Education. This book was edited by him in his private capacity and no official support or endorsement by the Office of Education is intended or should be inferred.

Library of Congress Catalog Card Number: 67-24098

ISBN: 0-448-05054-4 (WONDER EDITION)
ISBN: 0-448-04053-0 (TRADE EDITION)
ISBN: 0-448-03853-6 (LIBRARY EDITION)

1983 PRINTING

Copyright © 1964, 1967, 1969, 1971, 1975, by Grosset & Dunlap, Inc.
All rights reserved under International and Pan-American Copyright Conventions.
Published simultaneously in Canada.   Printed in the United States of America.

Contents

A space traveler will always see more water than land on earth from whatever direction he approaches our planet, or whenever he observes it during his orbit in outer space.

Oceanography—The Science of the Sea

"Water, water everywhere . . ." That is

Why is the ocean often called the "mysterious sea"?

how our planet looks to the astronauts as they circle it in outer space. And there is good reason for this: almost three-fourths of the earth's surface is covered by water. It is hard to believe that all our cities, farmlands, meadows, forests, deserts, and moun-

tains take up only one quarter of our planet's area, but it is true. For this reason, earth is often referred to by scientists as the *water planet*.

Throughout history, the ocean has greatly influenced the affairs of men. It has served as a barrier, as a battlefield, and as a highway for commerce. It has always been a source of food. In modern times, there is even more need

to investigate the sea as an expanding population threatens to exhaust the resources of the land. President John F. Kennedy once stated to the U.S. Congress, "Knowledge of the ocean is more than a matter of curiosity. Our very survival may hinge on it."

Yet the study of the ocean has always been a neglected science. Until our present era, we took it for granted that nothing much was in it. Our present limited knowledge has only helped us to understand the great potential of the sea. Until late 1969, only about two per cent of the ocean bottom had been mapped. This was due to the difficulties of deep-sea exploration. But sonar, undersea television, and small submarines especially designed for deep-sea work, have changed this. At the present time,

Only quite recently, man realized how important and necessary it is to explore the ocean. One of the newest and most spectacular oceanographic devices is FLIP, (Floating Instrument Platform). A research vessel built in America in late 1962, it can actually flip its bow, as our illustrations demonstrate, from a horizontal position to a completely vertical one. The bow, carrying a marine laboratory, is thrust 50 feet in the air; the stern, containing measuring instruments (especially for taking soundings) is plunged 300 feet below the surface.

the oceans of the world are being mapped and explored at a rapid and ever-increasing rate.

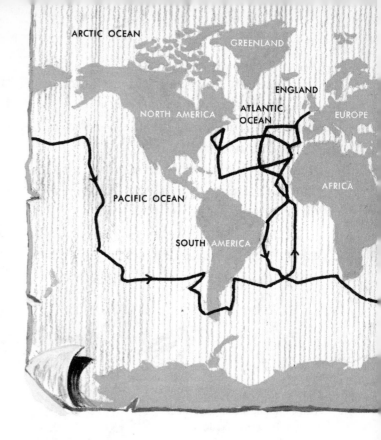

Oceanography is the name given to the study of the ocean. Oceanographers — often called the detectives of the sea — use the sciences of biology, geology, chemistry, and physics in their quest to solve mysteries such as where did the ocean come from; what effects does it have on land and the atmosphere; when and from where did sea water come; how many and what species of creatures live in the ocean; is it slowly drying up or getting deeper; and how can man make the most use of it.

What is oceanography?

The sea is a huge store of raw materials which has barely been tapped. Acre for acre, its animal and plant production could equal that of land, yet man at sea still remains essentially a hunter rather than a farmer. At the present time, only about one per cent of mankind's food comes from the sea. All the known chemical and mineral elements exist in sea water, some in great amounts, yet only salt, magnesium, iodine, bromine, and a few other substances are extracted commercially. Development of a good method of removing the salt so that sea water could be used for irrigation would transform millions of square miles of desert to farming land.

The movement of ocean water serves to regulate the climate on land and

Marine biologist examining samples of ocean water under the microscope.

plays a large part in determining both long-range and daily weather changes. The ocean's waves have sculptured the edge of the land and determined the outcome of great battles. Shorelines affect the passage of merchant ships. Great waves have taken many lives and have done a great deal of property damage. Below the surface, the modern submariner relies on knowledge of his surroundings to guide him through the dark, unfriendly depths.

Still deeper, the bottom collects the geologic history of earth. The pieces of bone and dust sink to the bottom to form layer upon layer of evidence of a long-past history. Such records on land have been destroyed by the forces of erosion. And in the ocean deeps, where the earth's underlying crust is thinner than beneath the continents, clues to the basic structure of our planet may be found.

To understand and find the answers to all these questions, to develop the

World map showing the voyage of the Challenger from the time she set sail on December 21, 1872, from Portsmouth, England, until she returned to port on May 24, 1876. She was at sea 727 days and covered 68,890 miles.

climate. In short, he taught the sailors of the world how to navigate *with* the seas rather than against them. His book, *The Physical Geography of the Sea and its Meteorology*, published in 1855, was the first ever written on the subject of oceanography, and it is still the basis of our modern science of the sea.

The three and a half year voyage of the British surveying ship, *H.M.S. Challenger*, was the first deep-sea expedition ever formed to study the ocean, and it set the pattern for most later expeditions. Starting in 1872, the expedition, under the leadership of Sir Charles Wyville Thompson, visited every ocean and collected thousands of specimens of the oceans' floors. The map drawn from these samplings of bottom deposits has not been changed much by the many subsequent explorers. The voyage also established the shapes of the ocean basins. It yielded the first knowledge of currents in all seas, and showed that the temperature of the water was fairly constant in all seasons of the year. The expedition of the *Challenger* demonstrated that the oceans were filled with unknown life waiting to be classified. It proved beyond question that life existed at great depths in the sea. The voyage of the *Challenger* established the methods of research for the great new field of oceanography. Unfortunately, almost 75 years passed before any amount of follow-up work was done on the information obtained from this voyage.

Why was the voyage of the *Challenger* important to oceanography?

vast resources, or even to consider seriously the possibilities of climate control, it is necessary to study the ocean, the life within it, the air above it, and the bottom below it. The science of oceanography is based on such study.

Interest in the ocean is, of course, by no means new. Men have been writing and telling sea stories since even before 800 B.C. when the Greek poet Homer described the adventures of Odysseus. But it was an American naval officer, Commander Matthew Fontaine Maury, who in the 1840's and 1850's, first approached the subject scientifically. He charted the currents of the ocean and proved that these immense streams have stability and direction and that they have a great influence on the

Who is called the "father of oceanography"?

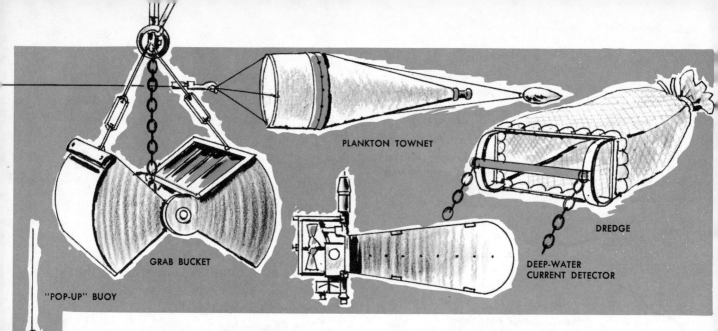

PLANKTON TOWNET

DREDGE

GRAB BUCKET

DEEP-WATER
CURRENT DETECTOR

"POP-UP" BUOY

DRIFT
BOTTLE

How Oceanographers Study the Sea

Nearly all the American scientists who

How is modern oceanographic research conducted?

concern themselves with marine science are on the staffs of marine and oceanographic laboratories, which is the principal source of employment in oceanography. These seashore laboratories, plus the research ships attached to them, conduct investigations in all aspects of the two major branches of the science: *geophysical oceanography* and *marine biology*.

The geophysical oceanographer studies such things as oceanic circulation, tides, waves, and physical properties of ocean basins and of sea water. The marine biologist, on the other hand, studies the animal and vegetable organisms that live in the sea.

The oceanographer is faced with many special and difficult problems when he goes to sea. The vastness of the ocean itself makes any observational program expensive and time-consuming. It is possible, with specially designed depth cameras, to photograph portions of the ocean's basin. But even a good photograph shows such a very small bit of random data that it does not give a clear picture of the ocean's basin as a whole. It is like trying to decide what your whole town or city looks like by photographing an ant hill in your backyard.

Because of the high cost of ship time and the difficulty of working at sea, the oceanographer puts a premium on simplicity, ruggedness, and the reliability of his instruments. These instruments or tools of the oceanographer can be divided into general classes or groups: those used for making measurements; those employed in collecting study specimens; and those that allow the oceanographer to go below the surface of the ocean for personal observation.

Measuring the depth of water, or taking

What types of instruments are used for making measurements?

soundings, has been done by man ever since the first ships sailed. In the early days, this was done by lowering a heavily weighted line to the sea's bottom. But imagine the difficulty of handling a rope to any great depth. When the crew of the *Challenger* made its famous sounding of 2,435 fathoms in the Pacific, it took them two and a half hours to let out the rope carrying the weight or lead and haul it in again. (A fathom is a nautical measure of depth equal to six feet.) Later, wire cable — which was easier to reel in and out — was used instead of rope. To take a single measure or sounding was still a difficult and time-consuming job. It is not surprising that only a few scientific-minded sailors like Commander Maury and Sir Charles Thompson were willing to take the trouble of measuring and charting the depths of the ocean.

Today, most sounding depends on the timing of an echo. Sonic waves are sent from a ship's transmitter to the ocean bottom; the echo waves return and are picked up by a sensitive receiver. The deeper the water, the longer

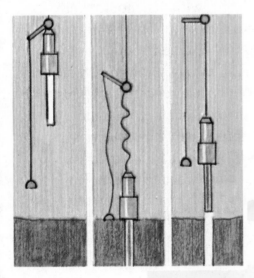

Oceanographers sample bottom debris with a corer.

How the core-sampler works.

the time required for the echo to return. The sounding machine, called a *fathometer,* automatically figures depth according to the elapsed time interval. Some of the more advanced fathometers simultaneously make maps of the ocean floor which show not only whether the underwater area is mountainous or level, but also the location of wrecks and schools of fish. If the *Challenger* had used modern equipment, it would have taken only about six seconds to record its 2,435 fathom reading. (See page 31.)

Fathometers indicate the depths of the *apparent* bottom. The *real* or rock bottom is often covered by many feet of sediment. To measure the depth of the real bottom, or the amount of sediment, the oceanographer must use *seismic soundings.* From one ship, an explosive depth charge is set off which creates earthquake waves in the sea bed. A special microphone, called a *hydrophone,* 10 to 25 miles away on the second ship, picks up the echoes of these waves, first from the top of the sediment layer, then from the rock layer's bottom. The second echoes give the measure of the real bottom, while the difference in arrival time of these waves gives the thickness of the layer of sediment. (See page 31.)

A new sounding system, used by oil companies, is more accurate. It also protects the environment. Hydraulically operated vibrations send synchronized signals which penetrate the ocean floor and send back reflections from rock structures. A *geophone,* located in a flexible cable towed behind the research ship, receives the signals and calculates depths.

Samplings of plankton (minute plant and animal life), fish, and bottom sediment are still obtained much as they were obtained

What types of instruments are used to take samplings?

aboard H.M.S. *Challenger* in the early 1870's, with *dredges, trawls, nets, grab buckets,* and *coring tubes.*

The *dredge* is a heavy metal frame with a net fastened to it. The lower edge of this frame digs into the sea bottom, loosening plant and animal life and passing it back into the net.

The *trawl* is a large open-mouthed net pulled slowly through the water by a ship. It can travel close to the sea bottom to catch some of the more speedy animals that can escape the dredge, or it can be pulled through the water at any other desired depth. Both dredge and trawl are similar to those used by commercial fishermen, although the size of the mesh is sometimes quite small.

The *plankton townet* is a cone-shaped cloth bag with its mouth held open by a metal ring, and with a metal can or glass jar fastened to the small end of the bag. The bag is towed behind a ship at slow speed to catch various plankton in the can or jar container.

Bottom samples are often taken by a *grab-bucket.* This device is shaped like a clam shell with two cup-like halves. Upon touching the bottom, a powerful spring snaps the jaws shut, and a sample of the ocean floor is enclosed and can be brought to the surface.

Still another device for sampling the bottom is a *coring tube.* This is simply a hollow tube that is lowered until it hits the bottom in an upright position. Then, the tube is driven into the bottom by the use of heavy weights or an explosive so that a portion of bottom is forced up into it. When the tube is brought to the surface and opened, the bottom is in its actual form, layer by layer. With the help of such instruments and the samplings they yield, the oceanographer can study the nature of the ocean floor from aboard ship or in his laboratory on shore.

Samples of the ocean water itself can be taken in *Nansen bottles,* named for the Scandinavian explorer-oceanographer, Fridtjof Nansen, who invented them. The cylindrical metal bottle is open at both ends, but has caps or seals that can be closed automatically. When attached to a wire and submerged, water flows freely through the bottle until it has reached the desired depth. A weight is dropped down the wire to trip a device which closes the top and bottom of the bottle, trapping the water within it. When this happens, the bottle turns over and this movement fixes the mercury column in a thermometer fastened to the outside of the bottle. The thermometer thus records the temperature of the water at the instant when the bottle was turned over. In this way, the temperature of the ocean at any depth can be measured. As a rule, a number of such bottles are employed at the same time at various depths. Each bottle, as it closes, releases a second weight which drops to the bottle below, repeating the process.

How are ocean currents studied? Formerly, the most common way of tracing direction and speed of ocean currents was by means of *drift bottles.* These were thrown into the sea containing notes requesting finders to mail them back to those who set them adrift. But bottles now have been replaced by electrical and electronic gear. Buoys containing radio equipment drift in the currents and broadcast signals to two or more ships which plot the paths of the buoys — and, consequently, of the currents — on maps. Or, one or more *flowmeters* are suspended from a cable beneath an anchored buoy. The flowmeters, which are free to turn in the direction of the current, have propellers spun by the moving water. Information on the speed at which the propellers turn and the direction in which the meters face is transmitted electrically to the buoy. All of the information thus obtained is then broadcast to ship or shore stations.

The techniques of underwater photography have been steadily improved and some remarkable pictures of the ocean bottom have been made. Stereoscopic time-lapse cameras loaded with color film are used to obtain almost continuous three-dimensional views of the terrain over which a ship is drifting. Underwater cameras are also used with various bottom-sampling devices or to photograph marine life. In the pitch blackness of the depths, of course, bright lights are needed for photographs except when luminescent creatures are the subject.

The modern oceanographer frequently relies on airborne equipment. Aerial cameras are used to obtain time-lapse movies of the development of clouds, or of changes wrought along a shoreline by storms and other forces. The airborne heat thermometer can measure the surface temperature of the

NANSEN
(REVERSING)
BOTTLES

11

sea and locate oceanic currents. The oceanographer of today is always working to perfect his tools in the hope of finding out more about the sea.

One of the best ways for an oceanographer to study the ocean's ways and life is to go below its surface for personal observation. Unfortunately for the oceanographer, man is adapted to life in the air. The lack of air, the tremendous underwater pressure, the darkness, and the cold have all combined to prevent him from penetrating, for a great length of time, the deep ocean to observe it first hand. In recent years, however, the development of

How do oceanographers go below the surface for observation?

Scuba diver with a Sea-Tow, a propeller-driven motor which pulls diver along.

Diver in traditional diving suit can safely reach depths of about 450 to 600 feet. He can move with freedom, but depends on a surface source for air.

suitable equipment has to some degree resolved these problems.

There are ways in which the oceanographer can go beneath the surface of the ocean. One is with his diving equipment; the other is in a specially designed underwater craft. Diving equipment, to be suitable for its task, must serve two important functions. It must supply the diver with sufficient air to breathe when underwater, and it must protect him against water pressure while permitting him to move about. To date, no diving apparatus that eliminates these difficulties has been developed.

The traditional diving suit with heavy metal helmet is suitable for depths of about 450 feet. The record descent in this type of suit is approximately 600 feet. While the diver can move about

A battery-driven diving vehicle with a scuba diver astride.

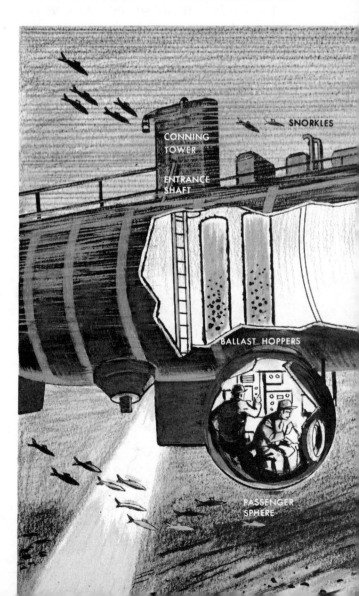

AIR TANK

with some freedom, he must depend on a surface source of air. For unlimited freedom of movements, the use of an aqualung or scuba (self-contained underwater breathing apparatus) is best. Instead of depending upon a surface source of air, the scuba diver employs tanks of compressed air which are strapped to his back. Thus, he is no longer dependent on the surface and at once becomes part of the water world. While "free" divers, as scuba divers are sometimes called, have made descents to depths of more than 300 feet, the average range of this apparatus limits the oceanographer to depths of between 200 and 250 feet. Diving with scuba equipment has become a very popular world-wide sport.

Scientists are working to develop a device that will enable divers to breathe the air dissolved in ocean water. If successful, such a device will make it possible for a diver to stay under water without having to worry about how long the supply of oxygen will last, thus increasing the potential for exploration.

To go deeper than diving apparatus will permit, oceanographers use specially designed craft to protect them from the great pressure of deep water. The first device of this type, the *bathysphere,* was made in 1930, and was used by Dr. William Beebe to study and photograph deep sea life. A hollow, heavy metal ball made to resist the pressure of the water was lowered from a "mother ship" on a very long cable. Alongside it was an electric cable for light and power and a telephone wire for communication. At the end of the

dive, the underwater craft had to be hauled up again by the cable. While dives to depths of 3,028 feet were made in this craft, it was not too successful because practically no freedom of movement for exploration was possible.

The most successful depth ship to date has been the *bathyscaphe,* derived from two Greek words, "bathy" and "skaphe," meaning "deep boat." It was designed by a Swiss professor, Dr. Auguste Piccard, in 1948.

The bathyscaphe moves up and down under its own power, and does not need to be suspended from a cable. The bathyscaphe also has a small electric motor by which it can be moved about over a limited area of the ocean floor.

On January 23, 1960, Auguste's son, Jacques Piccard, and naval Lieutenant Don Walsh made man's first descent to the deepest point of any ocean on earth — the Mariana Trench, off Guam Island — within the bathyscaphe *Trieste*. The depth of the dive is recorded as 5,966 fathoms — nearly 35,800 feet.

New types of manned vehicles for exploring the depths have since evolved, and more are being planned. The *Aluminaut*, a 51-foot submersible, creeps along the ocean bottom on wheels, guided by two men inside who also control the craft's long mechanical arms and groping claws which pick up undersea rocks and specimens for study. The Deep-Ocean Work Boat (DOWB),

considerably more maneuverable than the *Aluminaut* (yet also holding two men), can hover in the sea's depths for more than two days. Other depth ships include the 22-foot *Deep Diver*, designed by Edward Link and John Perry. It has a separate pressurized compartment that enables working divers to eat and rest at their convenience and then return to the water ouside without an otherwise long period of decompression. *Deep Quest* combines *Aluminaut's* size and depth capability with *Deep Diver's* "come-and-go" pressurized compartment.

Small mini-submarines, such as the *Nekton Alpha, Nekton Beta,* and *Nekton Gamma,* have been used recently for geological exploration along the Pacific coast and in the Caribbean. Weighing less than 5,000 pounds, they carry a two-man crew. They are equipped with high-intensity lights and manipulator arms.

Above, the bathyscaphe. To the left, a cross-section of the device showing its crew in the observation gondola.

Two-man submarines, also known as sub-surface snoops, are already in use for exploration of the deep.

Deep-Ocean Work Boat (DOWB).

How do men live under water for weeks?

The earth may one day become so thickly populated that men will have to find a way to live in the oceans. Experiments in living underwater are being conducted by men known as aquanauts.

In 1965, off La Jolla, California, three ten-man teams lived 205 feet below the surface in a large tank-like structure named *Sealab II*. Each team lived under water for fifteen days. Two men, one of them being Scott Carpenter, a former astronaut, lived under water for thirty days. The *Sealab's* atmosphere, kept at the same pressure as the water outside, was made up of oxygen, nitrogen and helium. The helium made the men's voices sound high and flat, like the voice of Donald Duck.

In 1969, four aquanauts spent two months in an underwater habitat called *Tektite 1,* 30 feet beneath the ocean in the Virgin Islands National Park. Air pressure in the living and working quarters was kept the same as the water pressure outside. This made it possible for the aquanauts to enter and leave without long waits in an airlock chamber for increasing and decreasing pressures. The aquanauts did not show any ill effects from living so long in pressure higher than that of the atmosphere. In 1970, *Tektite 2,* with 62 aquanauts, 12 of them women, got under way for the purpose of further investigating problems of underwater living.

The World Ocean

While there is a great deal that we do not know about the water that covers our earth's surface, we

What is the world ocean?

are learning more about it with each passing day. Thanks to the work of oceanographers, and their tools and instruments, we are uncovering answers to questions that have troubled man since the beginning of civilization. Such work is also changing many beliefs about the sea. For example, if you look at a map of the world, you will find that five great oceans are marked off: the Atlantic, Pacific, Indian, Arctic, and Antarctic. While geographers fix these boundaries to the world's water area, oceanographers have recently proven that there is only *one* vast ocean that covers the face of the earth. This they call the *world ocean*. All the so-called "oceans" we see on the maps and globes are really only parts of the world ocean. The continents of the earth — North and South America, Europe, Asia, Africa, Antarctica, and Australia — are thus only islands in this one huge body of water.

For easy reference, oceanographers subdivide

How do oceanographers subdivide the world ocean?

the world ocean into parts according to the depths of the bottom, distribution of living organisms, currents, climate, and properties such as the amount of salt content of the water.

Using the names given by geographers, most oceanographers refer only to three major subdivisions: the Atlantic, the Pacific, and the Antarctic. Some consider the Indian Ocean separate; others include it as a part of the Pacific and Antarctic Oceans. The Arctic Ocean, all agree, is really a part of the Atlantic. But, remember that all these "oceans" are only parts of the world ocean.

The Atlantic Ocean, believed to be named in honor of the Greek god Atlas, lies like a broad S between North America and Europe, and South America and Africa. It is over 36 million square miles (including the Arctic Ocean), and at its widest point, between La Plata River in South America and Africa, is about 3,700 nautical miles. (A nautical mile is 6,076 feet, while a land mile is 5,280 feet; or a nautical mile is approximately 1 1/7 land miles.)

The Pacific Ocean, a little less than twice the size of the Atlantic, covers more of the globe than do all the continents of the world combined. It is over 9,400 nautical miles in width between Panama and the Philippines and has spots that are over 35,000 feet deep. This ocean was named Pacific, meaning peaceful, by the Portuguese explorer, Ferdinand Magellan. In 1519, Magellan led the first expedition that sailed around the world. He called the waters "Pacific" because they seemed so smooth compared to the rough Atlantic which he had just crossed.

The Antarctic Ocean, often called

the Great Southern Ocean, lies around Antarctica, which includes the South Pole. It is about one-seventh the size of the Atlantic.

The Indian Ocean lies south of Asia and between Australia and Africa. It is almost round in shape, and is about 7/9 the size of the Atlantic Ocean.

Some parts of the world ocean are cut **What are seas, gulfs, and bays?** by points of land or by islands and are called seas. The largest sea on the planet earth is the Mediterranean, but even including its several arms (the Aegean, Adriatic, Tyrrhenian, and Black Seas), it is less than one-fifth the size of the Antarctic Ocean. Other famous seas are the Caribbean Sea, which holds the West Indies, and the Bering Sea, which divides Alaska from Russian territory.

Other portions of the world ocean are partly enclosed by land and are called gulfs like the Gulf of California, the Gulf of Mexico, and the Persian Gulf. Bays and sounds are smaller enclosed portions of oceanic waters and include, in the United States, the Chesapeake Bay, Long Island Sound, and Puget Sound. But, seas, gulfs, bays, sounds, inlets, straits, and ocean parts are segments of the one great world ocean just as villages, towns, cities, counties and states are parts of one land.

Many theories about the origin of the ocean have been proposed by scientists. **What is the origin of the ocean?** The most widely accepted one is that the earth at some time in its very early history became hot enough to melt the materials from which it was formed. While in this molten state, lighter rock-forming materials floated on the surface of the heavier ones. Then, between four and a half and four billion years ago, the molten earth cooled sufficiently to form a crust of rock that was many miles thick.

Surrounding the earth was an unbroken canopy of clouds miles thick and made up mostly of water vapor. Rain falling toward the still-hot earth was heated to steam and rose to the clouds again. After many millions of years, as the earth continued to cool, its surface temperature fell below the boiling point of water. Rain water could now remain on the earth, covering its whole surface except for the higher places on earth that had been formed from the lighter rock materials.

In 1970, scientists had pieced together evidence that the lighter rock materials had formed one huge continent surrounded by a vast ocean. Then, about 200 million years ago, the great continent began to break up, the pieces moving slowly apart.

The onrushing waters of the single huge ocean now entered and filled the spaces between the separating continents — and became the several oceans and seas we know today.

When water comes in contact with **Why is the ocean salty?** soil, it dissolves some minerals. You can prove this by taking a clean saucer and filling it with tap water. Let the saucer stand in a warm place a few days until all the water has evaporated. The film you see on the bottom of the saucer is made by the small amount of mineral matter that is ordinarily dissolved in tap water.

The early world ocean must have been only faintly salty. But, for countless centuries, rain and melted snow have been running over the land, dissolving various minerals, and carrying them down to the ocean. During all this time, the water has been passing through the successive stages of evaporation and condensation that make up the water cycle. (See page 43.) Pure water evaporates from the surface of the ocean and eventually returns to it, carrying various dissolved materials. Thus, the mineral content of ocean water has been increasing ever since the first rainfall.

When we say that the ocean is salty, we mean that its content of dissolved minerals is high. Sodium chloride (common table salt) makes up approximately three-quarters of the dissolved material in ocean water. The remainder is made up of varying quantities of chemical compounds, containing almost every known element. Some of these elements, mainly magnesium and bromine, are now taken from the ocean water commercially. A great deal of the magnesium used in the manufacture of lightweight alloys for airplanes and satellites, for example, comes from the sea. The amounts of the many other minerals in ocean water are so small that it is not yet commercially profitable to claim them. Scientists may yet find ways to make it worthwhile.

The total dissolved salts or *salinity* of sea water varies a great deal in different parts of the ocean. On an average, however, there are 35 parts of salt in every 1,000 parts of sea water or 3.5 per cent.

But, nowhere does the ocean approach the salinity of the Great Salt Lake in Utah (average salt content is about 28 per cent). This landlocked lake is believed to be the last remains of an ancient sea that once covered much of western North America. But, the world ocean in itself, at present, contains enough salts to cover the continents of earth with a layer 500 feet thick.

The upper layers of ocean water may vary from 29 degrees F. in the polar regions

What are the temperature and color of ocean water?

to a high of about 85 degrees F. in the Persian Gulf. (The salinity of sea water lowers the freezing point — which for fresh water is 32 degrees F. — to about 28 degrees F. for sea water.) Along the deep ocean bottom, the water stays at a uniform temperature of about 33 degrees to 34 degrees F. The average temperature of all the water in the world ocean is about 39 degrees F.

In shallow places, the ocean's water appears to be light green or muddy colored, while in deeper sections it seems to be blue, gray, or dark green. These colors change frequently, depending upon whether it is a sunny or cloudy day at the time. Oceanographers know that the water itself has no color; color in the ocean bodies is due only to the reflection of the sky or materials in the water. Some ocean bodies have been given unusual names because they are colored by plant and animal life living in their depths or because muddy rivers flow into them. The Red Sea, the Black Sea, and the Yellow Sea are examples of such names.

Ocean Currents

The waters of the world ocean are rest-

What are currents?
less. They are constantly on the move. Sometimes this movement is only up and down, while, in other places, it moves like the waters of a giant river. *Currents,* this general movement of ocean waters, have always puzzled sailing men. As you will remember, it was the currents of the ocean that first interested Commander Maury, and, through his research on them, the whole science of oceanography was started.

The oceanographer of today is still very much interested in currents, although a great deal has been learned since Commander Maury's time. There are two basic types of currents that modern oceanographers are concerned with: the oceanic currents and the tidal currents. Tidal currents, as their name implies, are water movements caused by the rise and fall of the tide.

The rhythmic rise and fall of the ocean's water is referred to as the tide. The tidal range in open water is about three feet, but as it nears land, it may vary from only a few inches to as much as sixty feet.

HIGH TIDE

LOW TIDE

Along most coasts of the world, twice

What causes tides?
every day, the waters of the ocean move far up sloping beaches, cover mud flats and marshes, and lift the water level of harbors, inlets, and bays. Twice, the water level gradually goes down,

The position of the moon and sun in relation to the earth has a great effect on the tidal range. When sun and moon are at right angles, their gravitational pull tends to cancel each other out, producing a very small tidal range called neap tide. When sun and moon are in line, especially large tides, the spring tides, are caused by the combined gravitational pull.

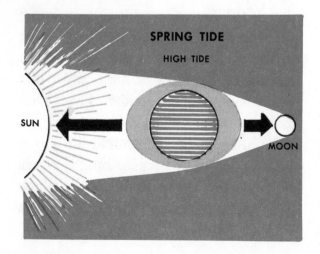

SPRING TIDE
HIGH TIDE

SUN
MOON

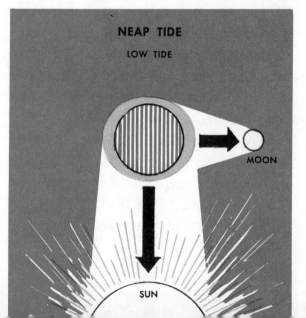

NEAP TIDE
LOW TIDE

MOON

SUN

exposing long stretches of mud, wet sand, and rock. This rhythmic rise and fall of the ocean's water is called the *tide*. The rising or incoming tide at its crest is known as a *high tide,* and the receding or outgoing tide becomes *low tide* when it has reached its maximum retreat. The incoming water is called the *flood* and the outgoing, the *ebb*.

While there are still many questions that remain unanswered about tides, oceanographers tell us their cause is the gravitational force, or "pull," of the moon and sun. While the earth's gravitational force attracts its own waters with a power millions of times greater than that of the moon and sun, their pull, acting on the ocean like enormous magnets, is able to draw the ocean waters into a bulge on the side of the earth to which each is closest. This water, piled up on opposite sides of the earth by the pull of the moon and sun, is known as the *tidal pile* or *bulge*. The height of this pile is called the *tidal range* and is equivalent to about the rise of water at high tide.

Because the moon is closer to the earth than the sun, it exerts the greater influence on the tidal bulge. As a matter of fact, the high tide follows directly be-neath the revolving moon. But, to balance this bulge of water on the side of the earth nearest the moon, there is another high tide on the side directly opposite it. Thus, the two great tidal bulges pass continually round the earth in a majestic procession. Conversely, the low tides occur in the regions situated at right angles to these piled-up water masses.

The position of the moon and sun in relation to the earth has a great effect on the tidal range. For example, when the moon and the sun are in direct line with the earth, together they exert their greatest force and thus cause abnormally high tidal range. These tides, called *spring tides,* occur twice each month at the full and new moons. When the moon is closest to the earth, we have exceptionally high tides, called *perigee tides*. When the moon, earth and sun are at right angles to each other, the gravitational pull is weak and the tidal range is small. Thus, these tides, called *neap tides,* are abnormally low. When the moon is farthest from the earth, the tidal range is again very slight and we have exceptionally low tides, called *apogee tides*. (See illustrations on page 20 and immediately below.)

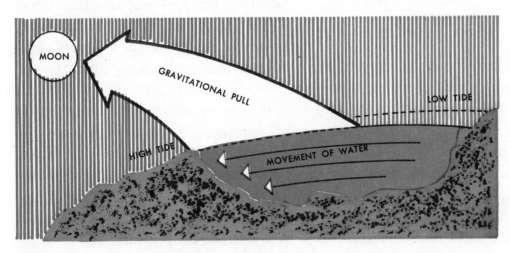

When one shore of an ocean has high tide, its other shore has low tide.

The tidal range varies in different parts of the world. In the broad expanses of open water, the height of the pile is normally about three feet. But as it nears land, it may vary from only a few inches to as much as sixty feet. The amount of tidal range is a local matter. The moon and the sun set the water in motion, but how high the water will rise depends on local conditions. The tidal range is affected by such things as the slope of the bottom, the width of the entrance to a bay, or the depth of a channel. For example, the tidal range in the Gulf of Mexico is normally only a few inches, but in the Bay of Fundy, an inlet of the Atlantic Ocean extending between New Brunswick and Nova Scotia, the high tide raises the water as much as sixty feet.

Is the tidal range the same in all parts of the world?

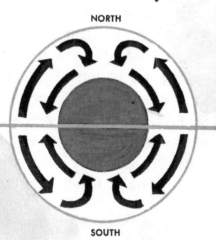

The sun's rays warm the waters of the oceans unevenly. This causes the heated waters of the tropics to move toward the poles in the upper layers of the ocean and polar waters to move toward the tropics along the bottom of the sea.

NORTH

SOUTH

The reason for this is the difference between the shape and size of the two bodies of water. The Gulf of Mexico is very large, with a gently sloping bottom. The Bay of Fundy has a very narrow channel between high steep walls. When incoming tide flows in the Gulf, it can spread out widely over a large area and thus does not have a chance to pile up very high at any one spot. But, in the Bay, the incoming water does not have room to spread out, and builds up very rapidly to great heights in the narrow channel.

The rhythms of the tide also vary. Oceanographers do not know why a few spots in the world have but one high tide in approximately every twenty-four hours, while the vast majority of the coastlines have two. But, they can predict exactly what time the different tides will occur, thanks to the use of special oceanography instruments which tell

NORTH

The spin of the earth has certain effects on all moving objects. It causes them to turn slightly to the right in the Northern Hemisphere and to the left in the Southern. Wind and water are affected similarly.

SOUTH

the exact pull of the moon and sun any place in the world. In the United States, the Coast and Geodetic Survey — a governmental agency founded by Commander Maury — prepares tide tables a year or more in advance and they appear in the leading newspapers along our seacoast and in some almanacs.

You can, of course, predict the time of tides fairly accurately without the use of instruments if you know the time they appeared the day before. The moon takes approximately twenty-four hours and fifty minutes to circle the earth, and the high tide will be about fifty minutes later than on the previous day.

Tides are important in seaports because

Why are tides important?

large ships must often wait for high tide before they can either enter or leave the harbor. For example,

The combination of three forces, the sun's heat, the spin of the earth, and the winds makes the sea currents circulate clockwise in the Northern Hemisphere and to move counterclockwise in the Southern Hemisphere.

Also affected by the spin of the earth and the heat of the sun, the trade winds drive the tropic seas from the east. The Westerlies drive the seas in the higher latitudes from the west.

in the largest port in the world — New York City — all big ships dock or set sail on the high tide.

Tides can have a great effect on saltwater fishing, too. On a high tide, the fish usually swim inshore into the bays to find an abundance of food on bottoms and banks they are unable to reach when waters are low.

Beach areas, which may be entirely out of water at low tide, frequently provide the best feeding grounds at high tide, when the surf or high tide churns up the bottom and uncovers mussels, clams, and other marine food. Weakfish, striped bass, corbina, flounder, bluefish, and others follow the channels and come within reach of the shore and bridge anglers.

Often, the fisherman will net his best catch approximately an hour before full tide to an hour after. When the tide is on the ebb, the fish retreat to deeper water at the outer edges of sandbars, or to channels that furrow the bays and inlets.

While tidal currents are the daily forward and backward motion of the sea waters caused by the rhythmic rise and fall

What are the rivers of the ocean?

of the tides, *oceanic currents* are the constant flow of water in the same direction. These currents are really the rivers in the ocean that flow along on courses that have remained much the same for thousands of years. While oceanic currents have no rocky banks or sandy shores to guide them as do our land rivers, they flow for thousands of miles through areas of comparatively motionless water. Some oceanic currents are so large and powerful that our biggest land rivers, such as the Mississippi, the Amazon, and the Nile, seem like little streams in comparison.

Unlike the rivers on land, no oceanic current has a definite source. Heat and cold, sun and

What causes oceanic currents?

wind, and even the rotation of the earth all play a part in forming and keeping these rivers of the ocean flowing. Since the sun does not heat the earth evenly, the ocean water in the tropics is quite warm, while the water at the poles is quite cold. Warm water has the normal tendency to expand and become lighter, while cold water will tend to become more dense and heavier. When the cold water of the poles starts to sink, the warmer water of the tropics flows out away from the equator to replace it. Thus, the heated waters move toward the pole in the upper layers of the ocean, and the polar water goes toward the tropics along the bottom of the sea. But, this natural movement of water would be very slow if it were not for the help of the winds.

If you were to look at a wind map of the world, you would find a series of winds blowing on either side of the equator, always at about the same velocity or speed, and always toward the west. Weather men call them *prevailing winds,* and claim they are caused by the fact that the earth revolves in an eastern direction. These winds push the warm, light water near the equator in a general westerly direction. If there were no land areas on the face of the earth, these wind-blown currents would move steadily westward around the earth on either side of the equator. But, there are continents and islands on earth, and

they act as solid walls that deflect these currents from their course.

In the Atlantic Ocean, for example, the *North Equatorial Current* gathers the warm water north of the equator and, under the influence of the prevailing winds, is driven westward. As the moving water strikes the West Indies, it is divided. While part of it enters the Caribbean Sea, another part turns northward, displacing the heavier and colder polar waters. This latter portion of the current is called the *Gulf Stream* and it moves past Florida and the eastern coast of the United States as far north as Cape Hatteras, off North Carolina. There it veers to the northeast to a point just south of Greenland, where it splits into three major branches. One branch flows northward between Iceland and Greenland into the Arctic. The second moves up between Iceland and Scotland and then past the Norwegian coast into the Arctic. The third branch bends back to the south along the coast of Europe and the upper coast of Africa, joining the *Canary Current*

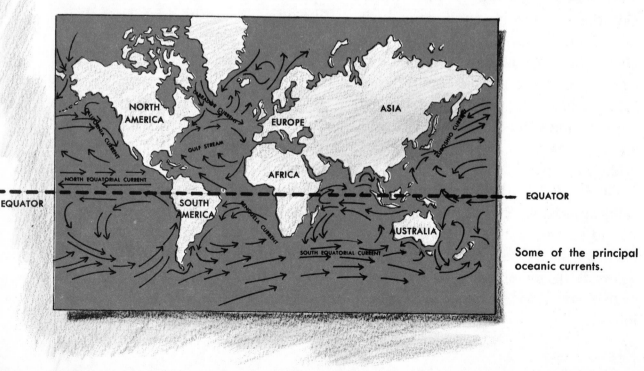

Some of the principal oceanic currents.

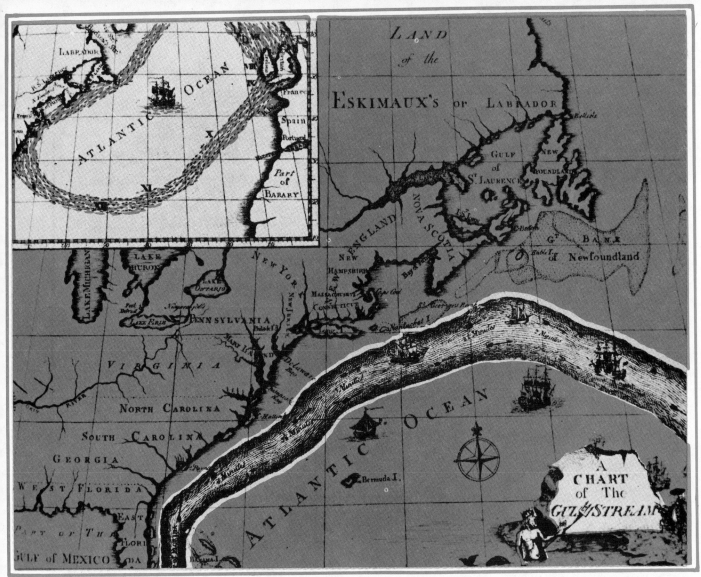

Benjamin Franklin studied the movement of the Gulf Stream. The chart he made of its course, temperature, speed, and depth saved westbound mariners about two weeks in sailing time.

to complete its circular path back to near the equator.

Where are the principal oceanic currents? There are major warm and cold water currents in all parts of the world ocean. In addition to the warm water currents in the North Atlantic consisting of the North Equatorial Current, the Gulf Stream, and the Canary Current, the major cold water one is the *Labrador Current*. This current, forming in the Arctic, flows southeastward between Newfoundland and Greenland. It continues in this direction, blown by north-erly winds, along eastern Canada and New England, and it forces the warm Gulf Stream to change its direction off North Carolina. However, because of its heavier, cold waters, the Labrador Current sinks below the Gulf Stream and continues its flow near the bottom until it reaches the region of the equator. Here, the water becomes warm and the current action stops.

The system of currents in the South Atlantic is similar to those of the North Atlantic, except that the open sea in the south makes the southern current, which corresponds to the Gulf Stream, much less regular in its path. The warm waters of the *South Equatorial Current* move across the South Atlantic near the equator to the headland of Brazil where the current divides into two. One part goes north to join the North Equatorial Current, while the southern half, called the *Brazil Current,* follows the eastern coast of South America down toward the South Pole. There, it joins the *Antarctic Current* and returns up the west coast of Africa as the cooling *Benguela Current.*

The currents in the Pacific Ocean are less definitely marked than those in the Atlantic because the Pacific is so large. The North Equatorial Current of the Pacific receives its drive from the prevailing westward winds and continues across the open waters until it strikes the Philippine Islands. There, it swings upward along the Asiatic coast past Japan toward the Arctic. This warm current, called the *Japanese* or *Kuroshio Current,* splits into two branches — one going on toward the Arctic and the other moving eastward across the Pacific toward British Columbia. There, it joins the cold water *California Current* and moves down the west coast of the United States to the equator. This completes the circular path of the major Pacific Oceanic current.

In the southern hemisphere of the Pacific, there is a similar oceanic current path but the exact path is less clearly defined so it has not been charted accurately as have those of the Atlantic and the northern Pacific. This is true, also, of the Indian Ocean.

Along the seacoasts of the world, **Why are oceanic currents important?** oceanic currents have a great effect on the climate. If you were to look at a map of the world, you would observe that the British Isles are just as close to the North Pole as is a part of Labrador. But the British climate is kept moderately warm by the Gulf Stream, while the inhabitants of Labrador live under a subarctic condition.

California partly owes its famous climate to the cold California Current. Without it, the coast of California might be as hot and dry as the northern part of the Sahara Desert; they are both about the same distance from the Equator. On the other hand, the cold Labrador Current coming down from the Arctic makes the winters of New England and eastern Canada much colder than they otherwise would be.

Ocean Waves

Ever since man first went to sea in **What causes ocean waves?** ships, the rolling waves have both fascinated and puzzled him. They are all over the world ocean. Sometimes they are smooth and gentle,

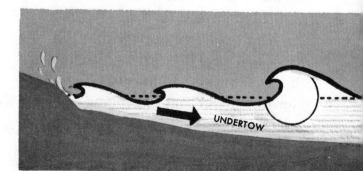

UNDERTOW

at other times high and rough. They have a thousand moods and tricks. It is the hope of oceanographers to eventually be able to predict and thus cope with their various behaviors.

Oceanographers, in their search to find the answers to their many questions, found that most waves at sea are caused by the wind. When the wind blows across the surface of the ocean, it pushes the water into "walls" or "rows" followed by hollows or depressions. The peaks of the wave rows are called the *crests,* and the hollows are called *troughs.* The distance between the crest and trough determines height of the wave.

Waves caused by a storm are referred to as a *sea.* As they travel away from the storm center, they slowly decrease in height, and extend the distances between their crests to many hundreds of feet as they roll shoreward. These long waves are called *swells* and they have a wave action, or rise and fall of the water, that is almost a circular motion. This motion does not, however, extend very far beneath the surface of the water. For instance, during a heavy sea or swells, a submarine submerged underwater will generally experience no water motion at all.

As the waves approach the shore line or shallow water, they are slowed down by the solid earth or rocks beneath, which drags at them like a brake. This causes the swells, or *breakers* as they are now called, to slow down beneath the water while, on the surface, they move along at their former speed. As a result, the breaker movement of the water becomes elliptical, and the distance between the crest and trough increases. The breaker continues to build in height until it breaks up into a roaring mass of foam called a *surf.*

The size of the waves depends on how strong a wind is blowing, on how long it blows, and on a third factor called *fetch.* The fetch is the distance in which the wind has blown without hindrance by land.

How big are waves?

A strong wind, blowing for many hours, may build up a considerable sea. Add to it a fetch of thousands of miles, and you will have some really big waves. An old sailor's rule of thumb says that the height of the wave in feet will usually be no more than half the wind's speed in miles per hour. For example, in a 60-mile-an-hour gale, the waves would be approximately 30 feet high. Generally, however, waves in the Atlantic seldom reach more than 40 feet, while those of the Pacific rarely rise more than 50 feet. Individual waves, of course, may be far higher. In a Pacific Ocean typhoon, single waves of more than 100 feet are sometimes reported. Such "mountainous" waves are prob-

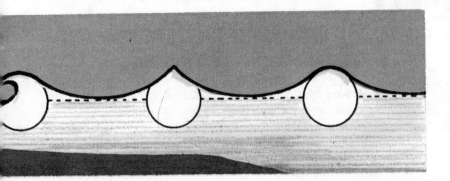

Winds pushing the water forward give the wave its rolling motion. When the wave enters shallow water, it breaks because the drag of the bottom shortens the wave length to twice the depth of the water. Thus, the wave is forced into a peak which breaks when its height reaches more than three times the water depth.

Waves breaking on the shore have enormous power, and a scene like the one at right is not an unusual sight on the edge of the sea.

ably caused by several wave peaks sudden piling up, building for an instant one huge mass of water. Waves can rise to a height of only one-seventh of their length before spilling over into white caps. The length of a wave is the distance from one crest to the next.

Wave action may continue in the water long after the wind that has caused it has died down. The reason for this is that waves always move much more slowly than does the wind which caused them.

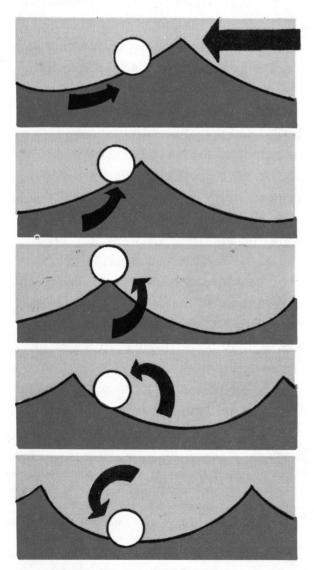

Does water move with the waves?

While the water appears to be moving, it actually does not. The water remains in the same spot, but the wave moves through it. To prove it, place a small piece of cork or wood on the surface of a lake a short distance from where you plan to drop a stone. As the ripples reach the cork or wood, it bobs up and down but does not move on with the wave. This shows that the waves are passing through the water, but they are not taking the water with them. Part of the water will move as the waves disturb it, but after the waves have passed, it returns to its original location.

The fact that waves pass through the

Watch a piece of wood or ball ride out the waves the next time you go to the beach. The position of the ball above shows how the wave travels and that the water does not move. The water motion goes from left to right, the ball moves slightly up the front slope of the wave approaching it, and then slides down the back of it. When the wave has passed, the ball will not have changed its position at all, except perhaps for a couple of inches.

water without taking it with them can be demonstrated by using a fairly heavy piece of rope about 15 feet in length. Fasten one end of the rope to a post. Now, move the free end up and down. The rope will form into waves and seem to travel toward the post. But you know that the rope itself is not moving away from you, since one end is fastened and you are holding the other. Each part of the rope is moving merely up and down. It is the energy of the motion or wave that is moving through the rope from the end in your hand to the end fixed to the post. In the ocean, a drifting boat moves because it is pushed by the wind or is carried by the tidal currents, but never by the wave action of the water.

Waves breaking on the shore have enormous power and a

What effect do waves have on the shoreline?

raging surf can be one of the most destructive forces in the world. It can break up the strongest pier, or pick up a house and carry it out to sea. It is the power of the surf that builds up and tears down the land along a coast. Waves make sea caves or sea cliffs, and cut out islands from the shore. They can also be beneficial in many ways, such as moving the sand in the ocean to build sand bars and adding land to shore lines.

While most waves are caused by winds,

What is a tidal wave?

a few are caused by volcanic eruptions and underwater earthquakes. When earthquakes originate beneath the ocean, and abruptly shock the waters of the ocean into action, *tidal waves* may form. These have no connection with the tide, and so they are not "tidal waves" at all. Instead, they are of seismic origin and in recent years have come to be called by their Japanese name, *tsunami*.

Tsunami, the most destructive of all ocean waves, may travel great distances before doing their damage. For example, the tsunami that struck Hawaii a few years ago taking many lives were the results of underwater earthquakes more than 2,000 miles away.

Tidal bores are caused by the blocking

What are tidal bores?

of rising tides on the seaward side at a river's mouth by sand bars. As the water gathers offshore from the sand bars, it builds up pressure which finally allows it to spill over the sand bar, sending a large wave or wall of water rushing up the river. Most tidal bores are harmless but the bore of the Tsientang River in China is often dangerous, with waves that sometimes rise as high as 25 feet.

The Ocean's Basin

At one time, it was believed that the

What are the three areas of the ocean bottom?

ocean's bottom was a huge, scooped-out hole which was nearly smooth. Now, thanks to the recent work of oceanographers, we know the bottom of the world ocean is divided into three distinct areas: the *continental shelf,* the *continental slope,* and the *floor of the ocean.* The continental shelf is a band of gradually sloping sea bottom surrounding all the continents on earth. Sunlight penetrates most of it to a varying degree. Vegetation similar to land vegetation grows here, and the bottom is covered with sand and soil washed from the land. Common species of salt-water fish are found here. Because it is shallow, most of our present knowledge about the ocean has been obtained from the continental shelf areas.

At one time, the 100-fathom (600 feet) line was generally accepted as the line of separation or demarcation between the continental shelf and slope. At the present time, however, most oceanographers mark the division wherever the relatively gentle slope of the shelf suddenly changes to a very steep one. The world over, the average depth at which this change occurs is at about 72 fathoms, although there are some spots off the Antarctic continent where the shelf ends at between 200 and 300 fathoms.

On the Pacific coast of the United States, the shelf is relatively narrow — not much more than 20 miles wide. On the Atlantic coast, the shelf is usually much wider. Somewhat north of Cape Hatteras, off North Carolina, it is as much as 150 miles wide; yet at the Cape itself and off certain parts of Florida, the plunge begins almost immediately.

Beyond the continental shelf, no matter

What is the continental slope like?

how deep nor how far from land, the bottom drops off abruptly. If you could descend to the continental slope, and oceanographers are planning to do just this some day, it would be a new and uncomfortable world. There is little light and no plant life; the pressure, cold, and silence increase; the scenery is mud, rocks, and clay; it is inhabited by large and small carnivorous animals, such as those encountered only in nightmares.

The continental slopes are among the most imposing features of the entire earth; they are the longest and highest

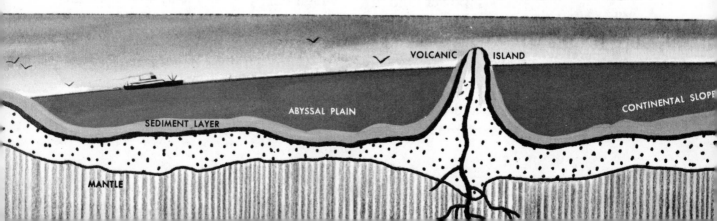

continuous boundary walls in the world. One of the most spectacular features of the slopes are tremendous submarine canyons with their steep cliffs and winding valleys. These canyons have been found by soundings and, in all probability, are of world-wide occurrence. Geologically speaking, they are relatively young — no more than a million or so years old. But how and why they were formed is a mystery.

There are dozens of such canyons or gorges along the continental slopes. The spectacular Grand Canyon could, in some cases, be dropped into one of these with hardly more than a splash. They are usually found near the mouth of a continental river. For example, the most completely surveyed submarine canyon in the Western North Atlantic is the Hudson Canyon. This extends from the 100-fathom curve, 90 miles southeast of New York harbor to a 2650-fathom plain some 300 miles off shore. This 200-mile long canyon is a chasm 1000 feet deep in places and has several sizable tributaries entering it. The canyon cuts through the continental slope and joins a depression in the continental shelf which marks the entrance of the Hudson River channel off New York harbor. In this instance, the Hudson Canyon system acts as a passageway down which sediment is carried by currents to the deep sea bottom which, at this spot, is an enormous plain of mud.

What is the floor of the deep ocean like? The ocean floor lies at the foot of the continental slope and is the true bottom of the ocean. This area, often called the *abyss*, holds the mysteries of a strange, unknown world. Actually, the floor of the deep ocean is the last

Our recently acquired knowledge of the characteristics of the ocean floor is based on the three methods we have of studying it:

1. The depth of the floor is measured by echo-sounding (see page 9).

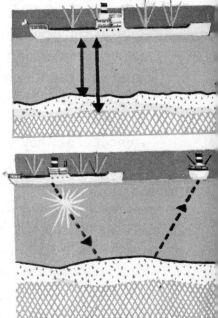

2. The composition of the ocean floor is deduced from seismic surveying. Sound waves from an underwater explosion are triggered by one ship. They are refracted and their traveling time is recorded by a second ship some miles away.

3. The general features of the sea floor are detected with echo-ranging. The difference between 1. and 3. is: in 1., a series of ultrasonic signals are sent straight down to the ocean floor; in 3., they are directed

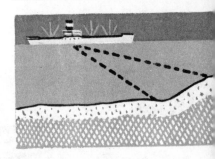

in a narrow, almost horizontal beam and actually sweep out large areas with sound pulses.

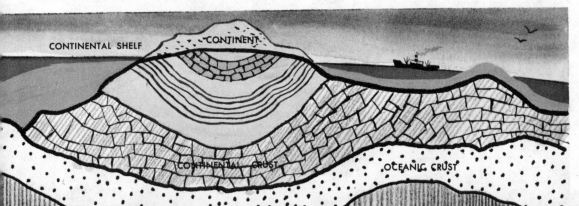

CONTINENTAL SHELF CONTINENT

CONTINENTAL CRUST OCEANIC CRUST

Cross-section through the crust of the earth.

31

large area to be explored on the planet earth. When we do explore the floor of the ocean, what we find there may be as amazing as anything on the planets in outer space.

Most of the work of oceanographers, to the present, has been done from the surface of the ocean. From various sonic soundings, we know that the floor of the deep ocean has mountain ranges, plateaus, canyons, valleys, hills, and plains, just as on land. But many mountains are higher, many ranges are longer, many canyons and gorges are deeper than land counterparts. Mount Everest, land's tallest mountain, could be dropped into the great canyons, or *trenches,* as they are called, and still be covered by a mile of water.

The average depth of the ocean is between 2¼ and 2½ miles, but there are spots where it is over seven miles deep. The deepest depressions occur generally near the continents. The Mindanao Deep, east of the Philippines, is about six and one-half miles deep. The Tuscarora Trench, east of Japan, almost as deep, is one of a series of long narrow trenches that border the outer rim of a chain of islands that includes the Bonins, the Marianas, and the Palaus. The greatest depths of the Atlantic Ocean lie near the West Indies and below Cape Horn. Because of these great depths, exploration has been difficult. But new research ships, like the *Seaprobe,* can search, core, and drill the ocean bottom in water depths up to 18,000 feet.

What are ocean islands? Explorers have, for a long time, realized that many of the islands of the ocean are simply the tops of mountains that rise from the floor of the sea. These mountains or *seamounts,* as they are often called, are usually found in groups or ridges just as land mountains are usually found in ranges like the Appalachians in the eastern part of the United States, the Rockies of the west, or the Andes of

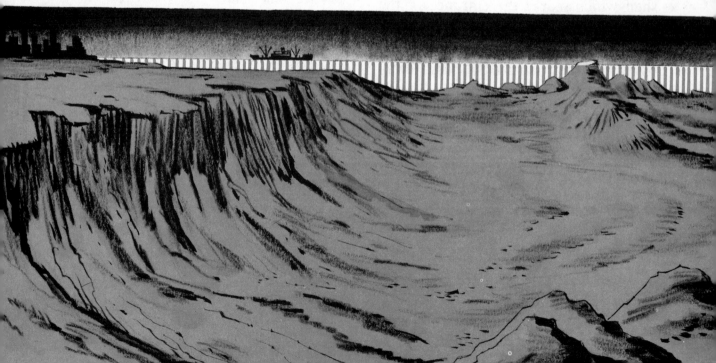

Atlantic Seascape.

Pacific Seascape.

South America. Most of the islands of the Central Atlantic, for example, are peaks of the Mid-Atlantic Ridge. The Hawaiian Islands, in the central Pacific Ocean, are peaks along the top of a great submarine ridge more than 1,600 miles long. The Marshall Islands in the western Pacific, are coral caps on great volcanoes. Thousands of other mountains rise from the bottom of the Pacific but do not quite reach the surface.

Where are the largest mountains on earth? Among the most interesting mountains on earth are the Mid-Pacific Mountains, a submarine range extending from the vicinity of Necker Island of the Hawaiian group to the vicinity of Wake Island. Material obtained by dredging and coring along the tops and upper sides of these mountains has provided clues as to their origin. This material consisted of pebbles, cobbles, and boulders of basalt, many of which appeared to have been rounded by the action of rivers or beach waves, and of limestone containing coral about 100 million years old. Geologists and other scientists concluded that, during the time when dinosaurs still roamed the continents, this undersea range formed a chain of islands.

At that time, the sea eroded the projecting peaks of the chain to flat surfaces. Reef coral larvae drifted to the islands, probably from the east, and lodged on and among the debris. In the warm tropical surface waters, enough of the corals grew and accumulated to form banks. There were not enough of these, however, to conceal the rocks and finer sediments (soil and mud) and thus form the islands or atolls.

Probably, as a result of adjustments of the earth's crust, the great range sank, at first fast enough to kill the reef coral, then more slowly until the present depth was reached.

The Mid-Pacific Mountains may be older, but the Atlantic Ocean has the biggest range of mountains. It winds

33

from the Arctic to the Antarctic with peaks averaging 10,000 feet. One undersea giant, Pico, in the Azores, rises 27,000 feet. Known as the Mid-Atlantic Ridge, this chain of submarine peaks and plateaus runs the length of the vast S-shaped trough of the Atlantic. The range, 10,000 miles in length, is about twice as wide as the Andes and several times the width of the Appalachians. The greater part of the Ridge is, of course, submerged. The central backbone rises 5,000 to 10,000 feet above the sea floor, but there is another mile of water above most of its summits. Rock-forming materials, welling up very slowly from below the earth's crust, made the Ridge. In 1970, scientists learned that this continuing process is spreading the ocean floor and pushing North and South America apart from Europe and Africa.

While there are a few spots on the floor of the deep sea where the underlying rock is exposed, the vast majority is cover matter which has settled from the water above. Oceanographers call this matter *sediment* or *ooze*. In addition to the mud and silt of every river on land that empties into the ocean, other materials make up the sediment on the bottom of the sea. Volcanic dust, which may have been blown halfway around the world, eventually finds its way to the ocean, floats for a while on the surface, then sinks. Dust from the desert is blown out

What lies on the bottom of the deep sea?

to sea. Gravel, stones, and small boulders, picked up by glaciers, fall to the bottom when the ice melts. Meteoric debris that enters the earth's atmosphere over the oceans finds its way to the bottom. But, as great as the total of this material may be, it is of minor importance compared to the billions upon billions of tiny shells and skeletons of the very, very small creatures which, for millions of years, have lived near the surface of the sea and then, upon death, have drifted downward to the very bottom.

Near the continents, on the edges of the continental slopes, is just plain mud — blue, green, red, black, or white — washed out to sea by the rivers. Farther out, the fine mud or ooze is composed primarily of the shells of the tiny, one-celled creatures called *globigerina*.

The sea floor over large areas in the temperate zone is covered with these shells. Over the ages, the species have varied somewhat so that it is possible to estimate the age of the deposit by the type of their shells. Although each shell is small, in number they have covered millions of square miles of ocean bottom, sometimes to a depth of thousands of feet.

The discarded shells of other living creatures also cover the bottom. *Radiolarians,* similar in appearance to snowflakes, form broad bands of sediment or ooze in the North Pacific. *Diatoms,* the microscopic plant life of the sea, are so abundant in the sea that their total weight is estimated at more than that of all land vegetation. The diatoms are one-celled bodies and they may be oval, boat-shaped, circular, or curved. They make up large bands of sediment in deep water. When this diatom ooze is raised up from the bottom and allowed to dry out, it becomes what is known as *diatomaceous earth*. This substance is used as insulating material against sound and heat, as a filler in making cement and rubber, as a filter, as a binder in the preparation of dynamite, and because of its abrasive properties, it is employed extensively in scouring powders and even toothpastes. Other uses of diatomaceous earth may be found in the future, as well as uses for some of the other types of ooze and sediment that are so plentiful on the ocean's bottom.

Until a few years ago, no one could have answered the

How deep is this sediment? question with any assurance. Now, thanks to modern scientific methods

The remains of small animals and plants such as plankton, radiolaria, diatoms, and many other such forms of life that once existed near the sea's surface form much of the sediment on the ocean floor.

such as those described on page 10, we have a fair idea as to how deep the sediment is. In some spots it is very thin and in others it is very deep. In the Atlantic basin of the world ocean, for example, sediment layers of 12,000 feet — ten times taller than the Empire State Building — have been found. No sediment layers thicker than 1,000 feet have been found in either the Pacific Ocean or the Indian Ocean and, in some spots, it has been less than 100 feet.

As the approach to the foothills of the Atlantic Ridge from the American side of the ridge begins, the sediments deepen as though they were mammoth snow drifts — snow drifts 1,000 to 2,000 feet deep against the slope. Farther up the Ridge, where occasionally the terrain flattens out into plateaus, the drifts increase at times to 3,000 feet. The peaks are bare.

Life Within the Ocean

The sea is the home of an astonishing variety of living

What type of life exists in the ocean? things, from microscopic creatures to giant 100-foot-long, 150-ton blue whales — more than three

times as heavy as any dinosaur that ever lived. In the life within the ocean, the oceanographer may find many of the answers to life on earth that existed thousands of years ago, as well as means to improve man's living in the future.

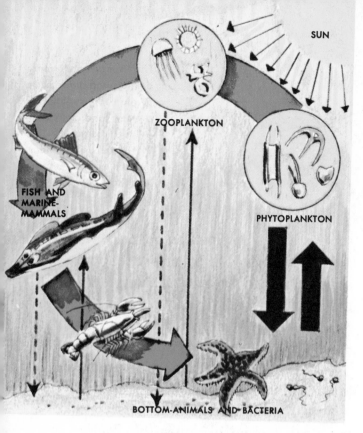

Life and food cycle in the ocean.

In the sea as on the land, the life cycle is supported by sunlight through the process of *photosynthesis,* the manufacturing of food in a green plant. The pastures of the sea are one-celled chlorophyll-bearing (green-colored) plants called *phytoplankton*. They are the food for the *zooplankton,* free-floating or weakly-swimming animals of many shapes and sizes. The zooplankton, in turn, feed the carnivores (flesh-eaters) of the ocean and, of course, the big carnivores eat the little ones. Death and decomposition complete the cycle. The organic material of both plants and animals is subject to bacterial decay which again releases the raw materials — carbon, phosphorus, and nitrogen — needed for the process of photosynthesis. Because organic matter sinks, much of the decomposition and decay occurs in deep water, well below the sunlit areas in which photosynthesis must take place. However, the essential

For this reason, nature's life cycle in the sea, and the way it works, is more important to the oceanographer than the individual plants and animals that live within the ocean.

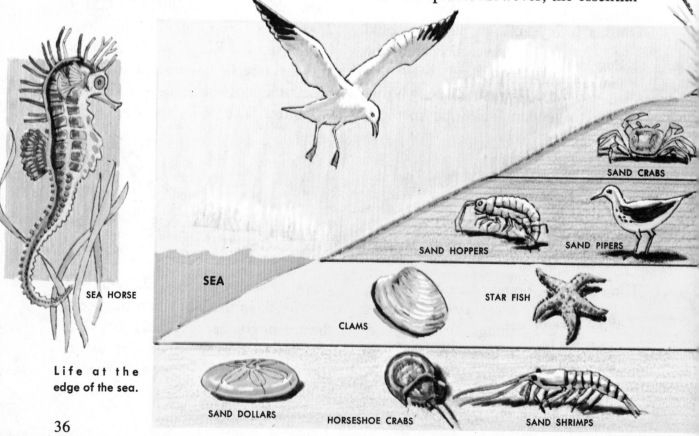

Life at the edge of the sea.

elements are eventually returned to the surface by oceanic currents.

Light sufficient for photosynthesis can penetrate to depths of only about 300 feet in the clearest ocean water. Although phytoplankton can survive only in these shallow areas, animal life has been found in all parts of the ocean, even at the bottom of the deepest part. At these great depths, we do not know how the life cycle is carried on, and may not know until man explores the floor of the ocean in person. We must remember that while a great deal is known about life in the ocean, much still remains a mystery.

The greatest population and variety of marine life is found close to the shore. But at the shoreline itself, the creatures of the sea exist under the most difficult of conditions. As the tide

What kind of life exists at the edge of the sea?

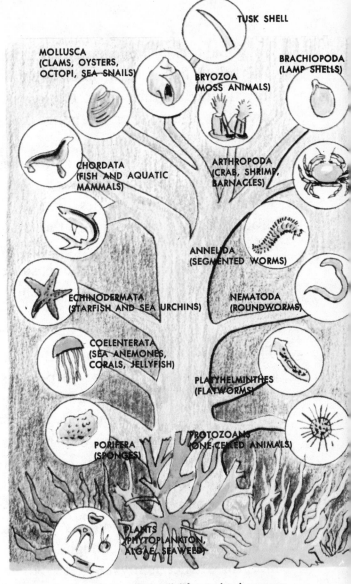

Life in the sea, from which all life evolved, ranges from the most simple, the protozoan, to the most complex forms of fish and sea-mammals.

rises and falls, they are exposed to drying, flooding, baking, and freezing. In addition, they must face the power and danger of waves. Most animals that live at the edge of the sea are streamlined or flattened, so that water rolls easily over them. Some, like the starfish and limpets, have suction-type devices which hold them tight against the rocks. Many, like snails and barnacles, can protect themselves by withdrawing into their shells. Barnacles attach themselves to rocks and pier pilings by using a spe-

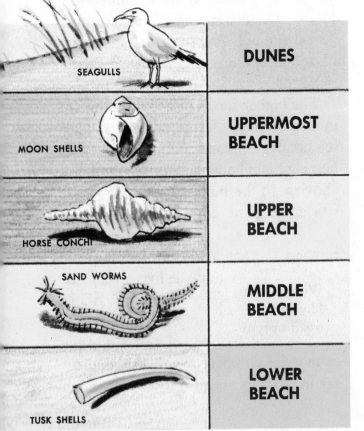

SEAGULLS	**DUNES**
MOON SHELLS	**UPPERMOST BEACH**
HORSE CONCH	**UPPER BEACH**
SAND WORMS	**MIDDLE BEACH**
TUSK SHELLS	**LOWER BEACH**

cial gland to pour a chemical over them. This firmly anchors them and there they stay the rest of their lives. Rocky hollows also offer shelter to sponges, sea anemones, and sea urchins.

The shoreline animals that live on sandy beaches, such as crabs, sand worms, clams, and cockles, find their protection by burrowing into the sand. While most sea animals will die if they are kept in the air too long, the seashore type can remain in the air from one high tide to the next.

The shallow water beyond the low tide

What type of life exists in the shallow sea?

level supports thousands upon thousands of species of animals and plants. As a matter of fact, most of the continental shelf is very well populated since plant life is able to attach itself to the bottom as well as remain within range of sunlight. Plants, in turn, attract many animals. *Algae* are the number one phytoplankton of the sea. They vary in size from microscopic single cells such as diatoms to the many-celled seaweed, which grows in the Pacific to the size of a large tree, 100 to 150 feet in length. In the matter of color, the algae also vary widely. On this basis, four color classes are well known — blue greens, greens, browns, and reds. They all contain chlorophyll and can make their own food. Algae can survive, as long as there is sunlight, in almost any kind of sea environment, as well as along the shoreline. The seashore types anchor themselves to rocks by means of a root-like process called a holdfast.

DEADMAN'S
FINGER
SPONGE

Except for algae, many one-celled marine bacteria, and some grasslike plants like eel grass, turtle grass, and manatee grass, the sea is relatively barren of plant life. While some marine fungi are present, there are no ferns, mosses, or other lower members of the plant kingdom in the world ocean. No highly evolved members of the plant family like the trees and flowering plants that are found on land exist in the sea. (See page 40.)

The smallest animals representative of zooplankton are the one-celled *protozoans,* of which the jellyfish are among the largest. Other members of this group include corals, anemones, a large number of tiny creatures and larvae or young forms of oysters, snails, and worms that live off of the phytoplankton. The more developed animals of the zooplankton include the *crustaceans* — crabs, shrimps and lobsters, and the *mollusks* — clams, oysters, squids, abalones, mussels, octopi, and scallops. These animals eat the smaller species of zooplankton and graze upon phytoplankton.

The higher forms of zooplankton are in turn eaten by all sorts of larger undersea creatures, from small fishes such as herring, menhaden, sardines, and anchovies, to the largest mammals in the world, the giant toothless sperm whales.

Beyond the shallow continental shelf,

What is life like in the open ocean?

animals live a very different sort of life; there is no plant life. In general, oceanic waters cannot be compared with the shallow sea in richness and variety of swimming

Sponges are plant-like animals that grow on the ocean bottom and feed on small water-animals. Before artificial sponges were manufactured, sponge-diving was part of an important industry.

SHEEP'S WOOL SPONGE

GLOVE SPONGE

GRASS SPONGE

life. In the open sea, food is scarce and the animals that live there find their meals at irregular intervals. Many animals in this region come to the surface to feed on zooplankton. Others, however, feed upon smaller fish or dead matter, which drift down from the upper waters. (See page 41.)

There are, however, some "regions of plenty" in truly deep waters. They are the oceanic currents. Marine biologists believe that only migrating or spawning fish such as the sea bass, albacore, cod, and mackerel frequent the currents themselves. But along the edges of these currents live the mighty marlin, the sailfish, speedy tuna, and other big-game fish. Such a location permits them to swim into the fast-moving current and grab a passing migrating fish for dinner.

There are also regions of plenty on the high plateaus, called *banks,* that rise from the ocean's floor. These high areas in the deep ocean have many of the same conditions that exist in the

shallow sea. Most of these spots offer abundant fishing grounds for the commercial fishermen; the three best known are north of Japan, the Newfoundland Banks off Canada, and Georges Bank off Massachusetts. (See page 41.)

The eternal night of the deep ocean is the home of the oddest animals that anyone can imagine. They look nothing like any of the other inhabitants of the sea. While most of them are small, scaleless, and flabby, their shapes vary greatly. Many of these deep-sea dwellers are snakelike, some are pencil-shaped or arrow-shaped with narrow fins running all around their bodies; others are almost as round as

What is life like in the deep ocean?

SOME OF THE MANY FORMS OF ALGAE

SEA ANEMONE

KELP

BARNACLES

ANEMONE

CLAMS

SEAWHIP

TELLIN SHELL

SEA GRAPES

LOBSTER

STARFISH

SAND DOLLAR

ROCK CRAB

LIME SPONGE

SEA URCHIN

ROCK BARNACLES

LIFE IN THE SHALLOW SEA

RED ALGAE

BROWN ALGAE

SEA LETTUCE

GREEN ALGAE

BATHYSPHAERA

SCARLET SHRIMP

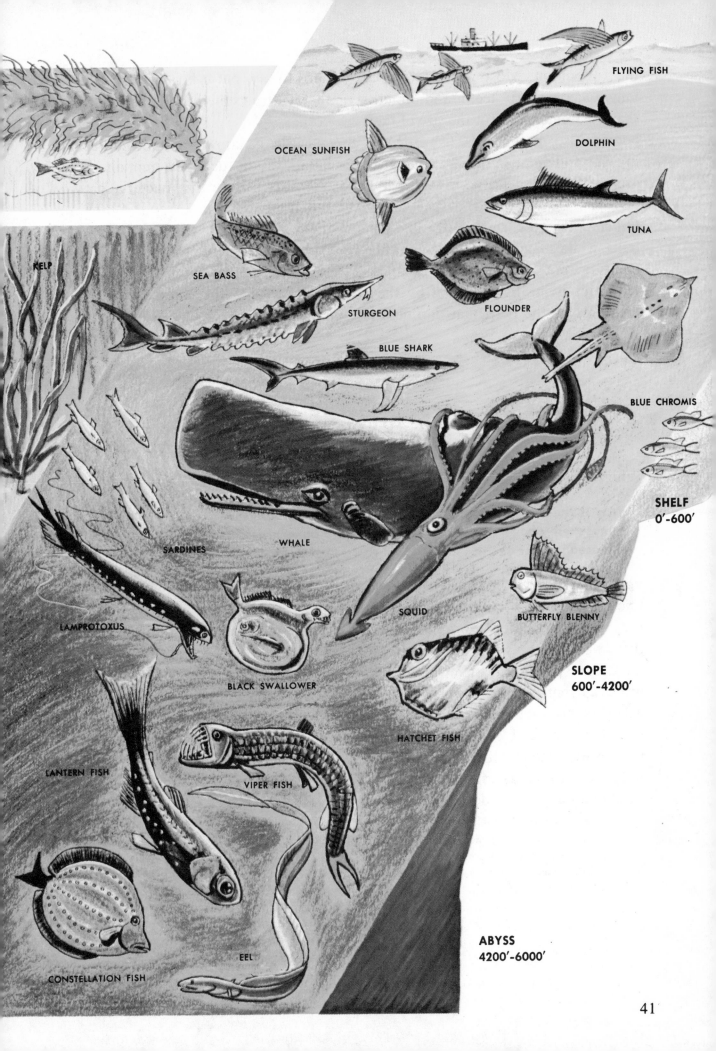

FLYING FISH

OCEAN SUNFISH

DOLPHIN

TUNA

KELP

SEA BASS

STURGEON

FLOUNDER

BLUE SHARK

BLUE CHROMIS

SHELF
0'-600'

SARDINES

WHALE

SQUID

BUTTERFLY BLENNY

LAMPROTOXUS

BLACK SWALLOWER

HATCHET FISH

SLOPE
600'-4200'

LANTERN FISH

VIPER FISH

CONSTELLATION FISH

EEL

ABYSS
4200'-6000'

41

the full moon. Most have developed long, needle-sharp teeth and mouths that are tremendous for the size of their bodies. Also, most of these fish are black in color and many in the deepest waters are blind, having no need for eyes in this pitch-black world of the abyss. Others have eyes which bulge like golf balls, while some have luminescent filaments or spots, which glow in the dark. How this living light is used by these creatures of the perpetual darkness is hard to say, but it is generally believed that it attracts their food, their mates, or both.

Little is known about the feeding habits of the deep-sea animals. Some scientists believe that bacteria provide the most important food source for them, while others think that they feed on each other. Like most other phases of marine biology, we are just beginning to understand the complex pattern of marine life. (See page 41.)

The Air Above the Ocean

Why is the atmosphere above the ocean important?

While the oceanographer is primarily concerned with the action of the ocean and life under its surface, he must also have knowledge about the atmosphere above the ocean. Without an atmosphere, there would be no wind disturbance on the ocean surface, no waves nor wind-driven currents; without the ocean, there would be no water vapor and the skies would be dry and cloudless. Without water vapor and clouds, there would be no rain and the land surfaces of the earth would become lifeless deserts.

Based on knowledge gathered by oceanographers, meteorologists are now able to predict our weather more accurately. At right, a weather man at work charting the track of a storm.

How does the atmospheric heat engine work?

The sun, air, and ocean water work together as interlocking parts in what oceanographers call the *atmospheric heat engine*. The power supply for this engine is the unequal heating of the earth by the sun. As the sun warms the ocean water, most of

the heat energy is consumed in evaporation or is absorbed by the water; the air above the ocean does not become greatly heated. The land masses on earth absorb only six-tenths as much heat as the ocean water does, and evaporation is less. Hence, the air over the land receives a greater share of heat than the air over water. This warm air on land expands and becomes lighter. Since the air over the sea is denser or heavier than the land-air, its pressure near the

The salt from a droplet of sea water that is squirted into the winds can become the "seed" which might release the rain from the clouds.

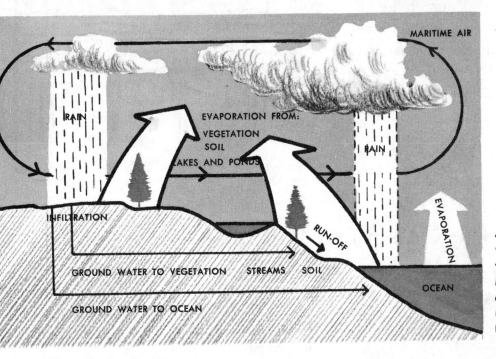

A graphic illustration of the *water cycle* shows how the working of the *atmospheric heat engine* prevents the oceans from drying out. (Based on illustration by U.S. Dept. of Agriculture.)

earth's surface is greater. This extra pressure starts it flowing landward, where it pushes the lighter land-air up out of the way. This results in on-shore winds, those that blow from the sea.

The sun's heat evaporates water from the ocean and water vapor gathers in the form of clouds. The wind may blow these clouds over land. When the water vapor of the clouds is cooled, perhaps many thousands of miles from their ocean birthplace, the moisture is dropped in the form of rain or snow.

Thus, the atmospheric heat engine could be called *nature's rain* or *weather maker*.

When the rain or snow falls, it either drops back into the ocean or sinks into the ground, feeds the streams and rivers, and eventually returns to the ocean. This over-all working of the atmospheric heat engine is called the *water cycle*. Winds and the unequal heating of the earth by the sun are also responsible for waves and oceanic currents.

Oceanographers and meteorologists

work together to learn more about the ocean and the atmosphere above it. Project GATE, recently conducted, used six orbiting satellites, 63 buoys, and nearly a thousand land stations that released and tracked almost half a million weather balloons. This 100-day intensive study covered 29 million square miles from almost a mile below the ocean's surface to the top of the atmosphere. Results from this study will tell us much more about the atmospheric heat engine and our ability to control weather. If we know fully how the atmospheric engine converts and utilizes its ocean water supply, it would be possible to change parched deserts into useful land.

Drilling operation for oil from deposits under the ocean floor.

The Ocean and the Future

New fishing methods: Fish, attracted by underwater lights, are sucked aboard by pumps.

What food do we get from the sea?

The prime purpose of the oceanographer's work is to obtain knowledge about the world ocean so that it can be used for the benefit of man. For example, he has learned through studies that the ocean is a vast storehouse of foodstuffs. But, at the present time, the only food that is taken in large quantities is fish. In countries such as Japan, fish form the most important part of the protein diet. But, of the whole world's protein available for human consumption, fish account for only a little over one per cent. With growing world populations to feed, however, it is certain that the world's

Salt can be obtained from sea water that has been permitted to evaporate under the sun's rays.

Settling tanks used in the process of extracting magnesium from sea water.

Valuable iodine can be derived from seaweed. However, the machinery is complicated and the yield small compared to the cost.

fisheries will have to increase their harvest, and we are sure that the sea can give this increase if we can learn better ways to gather and care for its resources.

Although the fishing boats use modern navigation, echo-sounders, and aircraft to spot their catches, they employ methods, such as lines, nets, and trawls, which have not changed for hundreds of years. However, as the needs of the world for food increase, new and different ways of fishing will be used. Today in the Caspian Sea, for example, fish are attracted by underwater lights and sucked aboard the fishing vessels by pumps. There will be efficient new methods, too, of finding the fish, thanks to many studies undertaken by marine biologists and oceanographers.

Through the ages, the larger species of algae or seaweed have **Is seaweed good to eat?** been used as a food supplement. Millions of people in the densely populated areas along the Pacific Coast of Asia and on the Pacific Islands — Japanese, Chinese, Filipinos, Burmese, Indonesians — eat over 100 different species of seaweed.

Algae of marine origin have been used for centuries as a fertilizer for farm crops and as a food for cattle. Several factories in this country process algae for cattle-feed. Seaweeds, especially the giant kelp plants that grow in the Pacific Ocean, are excellent sources of iodine. To process the plant, the kelp is dried and burned, and the iodine is separated from the ashes. Seaweeds are also processed into a substance called *algin* which is used in cosmetics, textiles, ink, paper, paints, and drugs as well as in chocolate milk, ice cream, cheeses, jellies, and jams.

At one time, the seaweeds were harvested by pulling it from the rocks by hand or cutting it by scythes on long poles. Today ocean-going harvester ships are powered through beds of giant kelp and can reap 25 tons in an hour. After it is gathered, it is dried out or dehydrated before it is processed.

As time goes on, the counterpart of agriculture in the **What is aquaculture?** oceans, *aquaculture,* will catch up with the latest agricultural methods on land. We will make sure that a great percentage of eggs hatch and that infant mortality in fish is decreased so that more larvae and young fish survive. We may hatch and raise small fish in controlled oceanaria just as we hatch chicks in a brooder or raise trout in hatcheries. We may also be able to cultivate the most abundant known source of life in the sea — plankton. Many scientists believe that both phytoplankton and zooplankton can some day be raised and controlled to feed the world's skyrocketing population. Whether or not this is true, only time can tell.

To obtain the full potential of the sea as a food source for mankind, it will be necessary to adapt to the oceans such routine farming practices as plowing and fencing. Plowing the ocean will involve speeding up the rate at which the nutrient minerals (the fertilizer) on the bottom are brought to the surface. Atomic reactors to heat the bottom water and make it rise have been suggested. Fences of air bubbles or sound waves might keep the oceanic livestock from wandering; air-bubble fences are now being tried to keep sharks away from beaches in tropical areas. New methods of harvesting the underwater crops will also have to be worked out. While marine biologists and oceanographers are not usually involved in solving problems of this sort, they work on the vital background information on which the answers may be based.

Making fresh water by removing salt

Can fresh water be obtained from the sea?

from sea water is already being done on a large scale in many places, but it is still an expensive process. But, with our ever-increasing demand for fresh water, scientists are working on ways to accomplish it cheaply. One method is to distill the water by boiling it off with the heat of nuclear fuels or the sun's heat and leave the salt behind. An electrical method whereby a current causes positive salt ions to flow in one direction and negative ions in the other, thus separating the salt, is another possibility. Also, there are thin membranes which let pure water through while blocking the flow of salts. Another method simply freezes sea water. The freezing process extracts salt from the water. After the salt has been separated from the ice, the ice is melted, giving fresh water. One of the best methods for obtaining fresh water, called multi-*stage flash distillation,* evaporates sea water rapidly several times, each time in a higher vacuum and at a lower temperature.

The wealth of the sea goes beyond mere

How will mining in the sea be done?

plants, animals, and water. It includes valuable deposits of minerals. Obtaining salt from the sea by evaporation is an ancient industry. Nowadays, not only sodium salts, but also potassium salts, are separated from sea water. Bromine gas, used in the manufacture of ethyl or "anti-knock" gasoline, is a valuable byproduct of both salt works and magnesium production. In the West Indies, converted trawlers haul in tons of squid, sponges, and sea fans, to be used in making antibiotics.

Ships in the Sea of Japan use what look like giant vacuum cleaners to suck up tons of shell and mud. Their prey is an undersea worm which supplies the basis for a valuable pesticide.

Other ships scoop rough diamonds from the ocean floor, while still others remove gold that is suspended in the ocean water.

Under the more shallow water of the continental shelves, we are now tapping valuable sources of petroleum and will turn to the sea more and more for oil. Petroleum, the stored sunshine of ancient marine animal fossils, lies not only under our land where the sea once was but also four hundred billion barrels of it, about a third of all remaining on earth, wait in reserve under the sea.

How oceanographers suggest mineral deposits be drawn from the ocean floor onto ore barges.

There are also some minerals such as cobalt, iron, copper, nickel, and manganese which lie exposed in plentiful quantities over vast areas of the deep sea. How they formed there over millions of years is not completely understood. But to mine them at depths of two thousand fathoms, some type of huge vacuum cleaner will have to suck them up into the holds of surface ships or submarine robot-operated, caterpillar-tracked earth movers will have to scrape the valuable deposits or nodules into submarine mine hoists.

Is the ocean becoming polluted? At the beginning of the 1970's, it became clear that human beings are polluting the oceans. Oil tankers and offshore oil wells spill great quantities of life-destroying oil into the seas. Coastal cities and thousands of ships dump garbage and sewage into the oceans. If something is not done to stop this pollution, the oceans will become vast sewers.

Our exploration of the last frontier on earth — the ocean — has really just begun. There is so much yet to be learned, and so much to still be accomplished. To learn all the secrets of the mysterious sea, we are depending on oceanographers — the scientists of the world ocean.

Acknowledgements: The author wishes to thank the following for their technical help and use of their illustrations: Woods Hole Oceanographic Institution; the National Academy of Sciences; the United States Navy; the United States Coast Guard; and Dr. Athelstan Spilhaus of the University of Minnesota.

THE HOW AND WHY WONDER BOOK OF
CHEMISTRY

Written by MARTIN L. KEEN
Illustrated by WALTER FERGUSON
Cover Illustration by DONALD CROWLEY
Editorial Production: DONALD D. WOLF

Edited under the supervision of
Dr. Paul E. Blackwood
Washington, D. C.

Text and illustrations approved by
Oakes A. White, Brooklyn Children's Museum, Brooklyn, New York

GROSSET & DUNLAP • **Publishers** • **NEW YORK**

Introduction

What are things made of? This is the big question which *The How and Why Wonder Book of Chemistry* deals with. There are so many kinds of materials in our world that the question is not easily answered. But for centuries people have tried to find the answer. The search has been long and fascinating from the time of the alchemists down to the modern atomic scientist.

Once it was believed that all things were made of some combination of earth, air, fire and water. Little by little new discoveries were made. Now we know that instead of just four "building blocks," there are at least 103 different ones! This *How and Why Wonder Book* tells how scientists have made some of the discoveries along the historic path of chemistry. And it records the answers to many questions that have always puzzled people.

More than that, the reader gets a feeling of the unanswered puzzles of nature which challenge scientists to continue their explorations. How is it, for example, that carbon, a common element, appears in so many forms? Sometimes it is soot from the chimney; again it is graphite, the "lead" in an ordinary pencil; or perhaps, most surprising of all, it is sometimes the brilliant and lovely diamond! Equally astonishing is that a green gas and a silvery metal solid may combine to make a white solid — ordinary table salt!

Of special interest to many readers will be several chemical experiments in the book, which may be done at home or in school. The experiments will enable young scientists to rediscover some of the facts about matter while working with materials the way chemists do. Whether chemistry deals with metals or non-metals, with acids, bases and salts, with foods, drugs, plastics, or with living or non-living things, it always goes back to one basic thing: *matter*. Since this book deals with many of these subjects, it is really an introductory reference work for all young students interested in chemistry. It is an essential title in the growing list of *How and Why Wonder Books*.

Paul E. Blackwood

Dr. Blackwood is a professional employee in the U. S. Office of Education. This book was edited by him in his private capacity and no official support or endorsement by the Office of Education is intended or should be inferred.

Library of Congress Catalog Card Number: 61-12932

ISBN: 0-448-05021-8 (Wonder Book Edition)
ISBN: 0-448-04023-9 (Trade Edition)
ISBN: 0-448-03808-0 (Library Edition)

1983 PRINTING

Copyright © 1961, 1969, 1975, by Grosset & Dunlap, Inc.
All rights reserved under International and Pan-American Copyright Conventions.
Published simultaneously in Canada.   Printed in the United States of America.

Contents

Early man probably got his knowledge of fire from the world of nature around him. From his observations of erupting volcanoes, and fires caused by lightning and sunlight, man soon discovered that fire could be put to useful purposes. Thus, he might be considered the first chemist, and it is a fascinating journey from that day to the role of present-day chemistry.

What Is Chemistry?

It is impossible to look around your home without seeing some of the things chemistry had a part in making. It was chemists who learned how to make the plaster that covers the inside walls. Perhaps the walls are painted. Chemists directed the making of oils and color in the paint.

Probably some of your clothes, the rugs, the curtains or the covering of your chair or sofa are woven of rayon, nylon or some other one of the man-made fibers that chemists have developed.

In the kitchen are foods that were bought in fresh condition because chemists made materials to preserve the foods

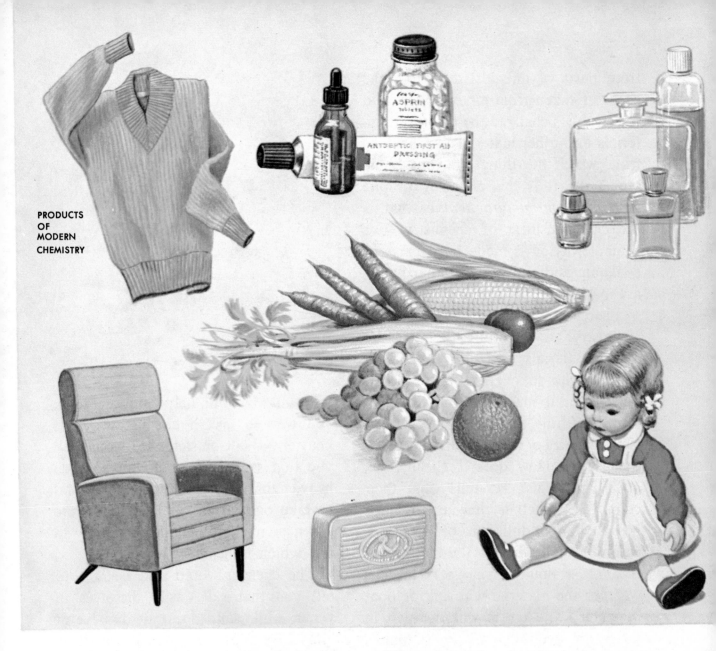

PRODUCTS
OF
MODERN
CHEMISTRY

from rotting. Chemists also made sprays that the food growers used to kill worms and other insects that might have eaten into the fruits and vegetables. Perhaps at this very moment some food is being cooked in your home. Cooking is a kind of chemistry.

In your bathroom are soaps and medicines that would have been impossible to produce if their makers did not have a knowledge of chemistry.

You probably have had toys made of plastic materials. Plastics would not even exist but for the science of chemistry.

If it were not for chemistry, the paper on which this book is printed would be a dirty, speckled brown, so that you could hardly read the words on it. And the ink in which these words are printed was made by chemists.

If you think about all these things in which chemistry had a part in making, you will see that none of them is found as such in nature. None can be grown on plants or trees, nor obtained from parts of animals, nor dug from the earth. Where, then, did they come from? Chemists took materials that *are* grown on plants and trees, obtained

from parts of animals, dug from the earth or taken from air or water; and the chemists changed these natural materials into other materials — the ones from which the things in your home are made. It is this *changing of one kind of material into another* that is the chief business of chemistry. For example, nylon is made from parts of coal, air and water, and some paints are made from parts of soybeans.

There is one other main task of chemistry: to carefully describe the many materials and their parts. A chemist who discovers or makes a certain material must describe that material carefully so that other chemists can recognize or make the new material themselves. How does a chemist describe materials? He tells what their colors are, whether they are light or heavy, shiny or dull, hard or soft. He is careful to tell whether the material is a solid, a liquid or a gas. He tells whether the material will sink or float in water, whether it will dissolve in water, in alcohol or in other liquids, how it will act when heated and many other things. These things are called the *properties* of the material.

Let us see how this knowledge might be of use. Suppose you had two glass jars, one filled with salt and the other with clean white sand. Suppose you did not know which jar was filled with salt and which with sand. You would not want to put sand on your food, so you would have to find some way of telling what was in each jar.

As you looked at each jar you would see that its contents appear just about like that of the other jar. So, just look-

ing would be of no help. Suppose, then, you were to ask a chemist which is heavier — salt or sand. He would tell you that sand is heavier, but so little heavier that it wouldn't do much good to take one jar in one hand and the other jar in the other hand, and try to feel which is heavier.

The chemist would also be able to tell you that salt easily dissolves in water, while sand does not dissolve at all. Now, knowing this, all you have to do is to take a pinch of material from one of your jars, drop it into a glass of water, and stir. If the material dissolves, it is salt; if not, it is sand.

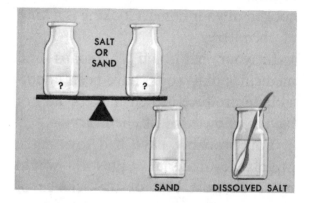

Salt will dissolve in water; sand will not dissolve.

6

Perfume was known in ancient Egypt. The picture, after a tomb painting, shows women preparing perfume.

The ancient Egyptians were casting bronze in 1500 B.C. The illustration, after a painting on the wall of an Egyptian tomb, shows workmen lifting a crucible to fill containers with the metal. In the background is a furnace, and on the floor, foot-operated bellows.

ALCHEMIST'S EQUIPMENT

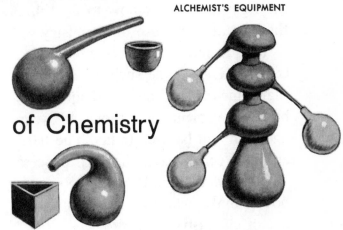

The Ancestors of Chemistry

Men were making use of chemistry long before they knew anything about the science of chemistry. For example, the ancient Egyptians, more than 3,000 years ago, had learned skill in working iron. This metal is found in the earth combined with other materials to make a reddish brown rock-like material. In this form, it is called iron ore. For the Egyptians to separate the metal from the rest of the iron ore required a real use of chemistry. The Egyptians and several other ancient peoples who lived on the shores of the Mediterranean Sea mined silver, gold, lead, tin and copper. They knew how to combine copper and tin to form bronze, a metal that is quite hard, but from which it is easy to make things.

How did chemistry begin?

Ancient peoples made spears, swords, helmets, bells, horns, chariots, chairs, pots, pans and a host of other things from bronze. To combine copper and tin in just the right amounts for making bronze was a skill that also required a use of chemistry.

The ancient Egyptians could make glass, tile, turpentine, soap and dyes. To make any of these things requires the use of chemistry. So good were the Egyptians at making them that some of their colored glass and tile have been dug up from the earth where they were buried for thousands of years — and the colors are as bright as when

7

The alchemists, the forefathers of today's chemists, tried to make gold out of other metals, searched for a drink that would give eternal youth and everlasting life, and sought a liquid that would dissolve anything. Many alchemists worked seriously to achieve their goals. The walls of their laboratories were covered with secret symbols, and many pieces of laboratory equipment they developed are still in use.

the glass and tile decorated the palaces of Egyptian pharaohs. Egyptian pictures in colored tile show ships with bright-colored stripes dyed in their sails, and nobles, both men and women, wearing beautifully colored clothes. All these facts are still more evidence that the Egyptians knew how to do things that required the use of chemistry.

The Romans knew how to make cement. They made such good cement that some of their roads and aqueducts, built of cement two thousand years ago, can still be used today. The hardening of cement is a chemical process. This shows that the Romans, too, knew how to make materials that required the use of chemistry.

Empedocles: all things are made of four elements

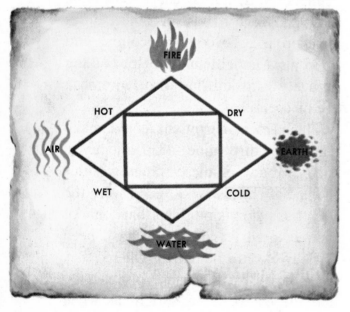

An ancient Greek wise man named Empedocles taught that all materials are made of four things called *elements:* earth, air, water and fire. For two thousand years after Empedocles, certain men tried to make different kinds of materials by combining these four elements in different ways. Fortunately, for the future of chemistry, these men thought of earth as including anything solid, such as ore, metal, salt, glass or wood. Also, they counted any kind of gas as air and any liquid as water.

Jugs of colored water, symbolic colors originated by the alchemists, are still used today in modern pharmacies and drugstores as a professional sign.

What these men were most interested in doing was to change cheap metals, such as tin, iron and lead, into gold. Where did they get the idea that less valuable metals could be turned into gold? The idea came from another ancient Greek, Aristotle, who had written that all things had the possibility of becoming perfect. Gold was considered to be the only perfect metal, and many people reasoned that less perfect metals could

How did chemistry get its name?

be changed into gold — if one could only learn how. And if one *could* learn how, men of olden times thought, what a wonderful way to become rich! The man who could learn the secret of changing a metal like lead into gold would soon be richer than anyone else. It was not hard to get hundreds of pounds of lead, but very few men owned even an ounce of gold.

The work of trying to change less valuable metals into gold was called *alchemy,* and the men who did this

9

work were *alchemists*. It was from these words that we got our modern words *chemistry* and *chemist*. Because of the work they were doing, alchemists were given the nickname of "gold cooks." In the courts of many kings and nobles, the gold cooks held an honored place. One emperor built, near his palace, six small stone houses with large furnaces for the use of the royal alchemists. King Henry VI of England told his noblemen and scholars that alchemy was a valuable study that they should all learn.

Besides gold, there were two other things that alchemists tried to make in their laboratories. One was a liquid that would dissolve anything. They never stopped to think that such a liquid would also dissolve any bottle or other container in which they tried to keep it. The other thing they sought was a drink that would make old people young, and would cause all who drank it to live forever.

For hundreds of years alchemists worked in vain, never discovering any of the things they sought. They worked in smoke-blackened laboratories filled with the strange fumes and odors given off by the liquids they boiled and the powders they burned. The stone walls were covered with mysterious signs that were supposed to have magic powers. The red light of the fires in the alche-

mists' furnaces cast weird shadows and made eerie gleams dance on the odd-shaped glassware in which the gold cooks heated and stored their brews.

Alchemists found that a number of materials were especially **What were alchemical symbols?** useful in their work. Also, they discovered some new materials. They wanted to keep their knowledge of these materials secret from all except other alchemists. To do this, alchemists devised a number of signs, or *symbols,* that stood for the names of the metals and other substances with which they worked.

Following are the signs that alchemists painted on the walls of their laboratories. Alchemists liked to believe that their symbols made alchemy seem mysteriously important to those who were not alchemists. In addition to the alchemical symbols are the materials the symbols stand for:

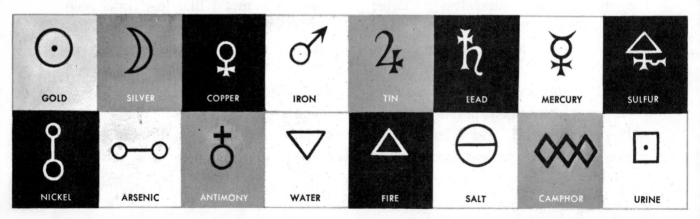

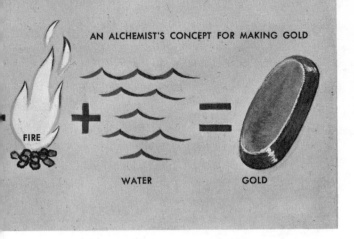

AN ALCHEMIST'S CONCEPT FOR MAKING GOLD

FIRE + WATER = GOLD

Some alchemists were dishonest. They cleverly hid small lumps of gold in their furnaces.

What happened to alchemy?

Then, in the presence of those from whom they got money, the alchemists "discovered" the gold in the ashes of one of their experiments. And then, they claimed that if they were given more money for more experiments, surely a way would be found to get really large lumps of gold out of the ashes.

Other alchemists were honest. In the hundreds of years of their fruitless experimenting, they gathered a long list of useful facts about their work. They described the ways in which many materials acted when mixed together or heated or shaken. They learned which liquids would dissolve metals and other materials, and which liquids would dissolve in others. They recorded the weights and colors and many other facts.

It is only about two hundred years since the last alchemist gave up his hopeless search. But the information gathered by him and the alchemists who lived earlier made up a store of knowledge, some of which became the basis for the true science of chemistry.

The Language of Chemistry

Every science has words that describe things and ideas with which the science deals. The words chemists use when they talk about their work are called "chemical terms," and they are important to know if we are to understand the science of chemistry.

Anything that has weight is matter.

MATTER

The first word is *matter*. When a chemist talks about matter, he means anything that has weight. Anything you can see or touch is matter. This book, your

What is matter?

nose, ice cream, a rock, water, milk, air, the sun, moon and stars are all examples of matter.

Are there any things that are not matter? Yes. Radio waves and television waves and heat are among the things that have no weight, and therefore are not matter. Also, ideas and feelings are things, but they are not matter. Patriotism, love, sadness, memories and daydreams have no weight and are not matter.

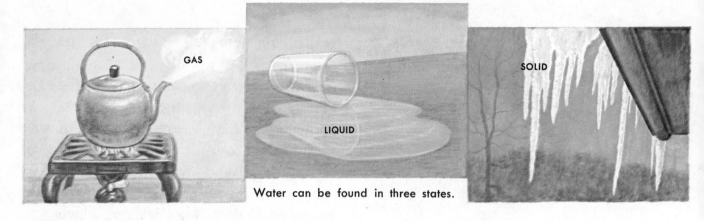

GAS

LIQUID

SOLID

Water can be found in three states.

The objects in the world about us seem to be made up of an endless number of different kinds of matter.

What are the three states of matter?

Things are made of wood, paper, metal, rubber, cloth, plastic and a host of other materials. There is rough and smooth matter, hard and soft matter — and all matter appears in a great variety of colors and shapes. There are millions of different kinds of matter. Yet, a chemist separates all matter into three divisions: matter that is *solid*, matter that is *liquid* and matter that is *gas*. Each one of these large divisions of matter is called a *state of matter*. A rock and a baseball are examples of matter in the solid state. Water, milk and gasoline represent matter in the liquid state. Air is matter in the state of a gas.

If you place an ice cube in a glass half full of water, you can see all three states of matter at one time. The ice is solid, the water is liquid and the air above the water is gas.

Place two or three ice cubes into an empty teakettle. Put the kettle on a burner of a gas range. Keep the flame of the burner

How can you change one state of matter into another state?

low and leave the lid off the kettle. What happens inside the kettle? The ice melts; that is, it changes to water. Here, you see a solid changing to a liquid.

Put the lid on the kettle and turn the burner up higher. When the water in the kettle boils, look at the spout from the side. Between the spout and the steam, you will see a clear space. In this space is *water vapor;* that is, water in the form of a gas. (Do not try to touch the water vapor! It is very hot, and will give you a bad burn.)

The steam, which begins to appear just in front of the water vapor, is made up of tiny droplets of water. Upon leaving the spout, the water vapor came in contact with the cooler air, and the gas (water vapor) changed to a liquid (water). If you want to prove that cooling water vapor changes to water, wrap a towel around the handle of a tablespoon and hold the bowl of the spoon in the water vapor. (Be careful!) Drops of water will collect on the spoon.

If you should put the water that collects on the spoon into the freezing compartment of a refrigerator, the water would turn to ice. Thus, you would have an example of matter in the liquid state turning to matter in the solid state.

Most kinds of matter can exist in each

of the three states. Iron can be melted and, thereby, changed from the solid to the liquid state. The iron becomes liquid when it is heated to 2,800 degrees Fahrenheit. (The usual temperature inside a house is about 70 degrees Fahrenheit.) If liquid iron is heated further, until its temperature reaches 5,400 degrees Fahrenheit, the iron boils and becomes a gas.

You have probably noticed the bubbles in soda. These bubbles are made of *carbon dioxide*, a harmless gas. If you were to put some of this gas into the proper kind of container, and then lower the temperature to 69 degrees below zero Fahrenheit, the carbon dioxide gas would turn to liquid carbon dioxide. If you cooled the liquid carbon dioxide further, until its temperature dropped to 110 degrees below zero Fahrenheit, the liquid would become solid. Perhaps you have seen solid carbon dioxide. It is called "dry ice," and is used by street vendors of ice cream to keep their wares cold.

You have probably guessed that by changing the temperature of matter, you can change it from one state to another. This is true. Heating and cooling matter are the main ways chemists use to change it from one state to another.

Tanning animal hides makes them into leather by causing a chemical change that prevents rotting. After soaking hides in salt water to remove dirt and blood, ancient tanners rubbed the hides with lime to remove the hair. The limed hides were washed and hung on sticks in vats of tanning solution made by soaking bark, leaves, wood or nuts in water. The leather was rubbed with oil to make it soft. This process has been replaced by new methods (right).

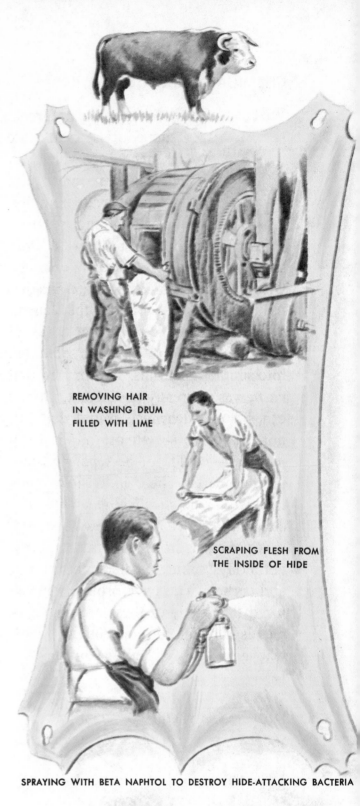

REMOVING HAIR IN WASHING DRUM FILLED WITH LIME

SCRAPING FLESH FROM THE INSIDE OF HIDE

SPRAYING WITH BETA NAPHTOL TO DESTROY HIDE-ATTACKING BACTERIA

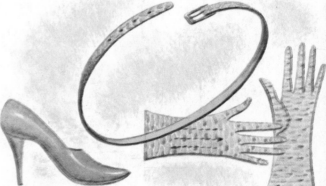

CHEMICAL ELEMENTS

What is a chemical element?

We have learned that the ancient Greek, Empedocles, said the elements of which all things are made are earth, air, water and fire. Now an element of anything is a part so simple that it cannot be divided into any simpler parts. When alchemists worked with various solid materials that they believed to be forms of the element *earth*, they soon learned that many of these solid materials could be separated into simpler materials. This proved that *earth* was not really an element. On the other hand, alchemists found that certain materials — almost all of them metals — could not be separated into simpler parts. These indivisible materials were true *chemical elements*. The elements the alchemists knew were gold, silver, copper, iron, lead, tin, mercury, antimony, sulfur, arsenic, phosphorus and carbon. You have probably recognized that many of these are names of metals known to the ancient Egyptians, who also knew of sulfur and carbon.

Mercury was probably discovered about the year A.D. 300 by a Greek named Theophrastus, while the elements arsenic and antimony were discovered in the Middle Ages.

In the eighteenth century, when chemistry was becoming a science, chemists began to discover new chemical elements. The discovery of elements went on until chemists had found 92 elements in materials gotten from the earth and the air. Then, recently, chemists learned how to make new chemical elements, and have made fourteen more for a total of 106 elements. On page 15 is a table of all the chemical elements discovered up to the time these words were written. The last three discovered have not yet been named.

Chemical elements are the simplest kinds of matter with which a chemist works.

CHEMICAL SYMBOLS

What are chemical symbols?

Following the name of each element in the list on page 15, you will see one or two letters. For instance, following *calcium* are the letters *Ca*. These letters are an abbreviation of the name of the element. Chemists find that using these abbreviations is easier

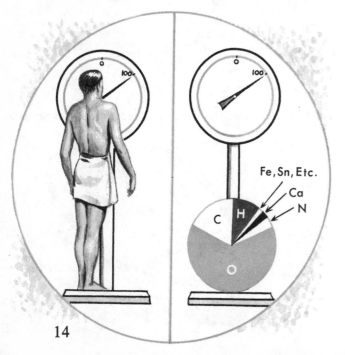

Fe, Sn, Etc.
Ca
N
C
H
O

If you weigh 100 pounds, your body is made up of roughly 65 pounds of oxygen, 18 pounds of carbon, 10 pounds of hydrogen, 3 pounds of nitrogen, 2 pounds of calcium, 1 pound of phosphorus. The remaining pound consists of iron, zinc, potassium, sodium, chlorine, fluorine, bromine, iodine, magnesium, manganese, copper, chromium, molybdenum, titanium, rhubidium, strontium, sulfur, selenium, boron, nickel, arsenic, cobalt, silicon, lithium, aluminum, tin, and barium. Altogether, your body has 33 elements.

Element	Symbol	Element	Symbol	Element	Symbol	Element	Symbol
Actinium	Ac	Erbium	Er	Mercury	Hg	Samarium	Sm
Aluminum	Al	Europium	Eu	Molybdenum	Mo	Scandium	Sc
Americium	Am	Fermium	Fm	Neodymium	Nd	Selenium	Se
Antimony	Sb	Fluorine	F	Neon	Ne	Silicon	Si
Argon	Ar	Francium	Fr	Neptunium	Np	Silver	Ag
Arsenic	As	Gadolinium	Gd	Nickel	Ni	Sodium	Na
Astatine	At	Gallium	Ga	Niobium	Nb	Strontium	Sr
Barium	Ba	Germanium	Ge	Nitrogen	N	Sulfur	S
Berkelium	Bk	Gold	Au	Nobelium	No	Tantalum	Ta
Beryllium	Be	Hafnium	Hf	Osmium	Os	Technetium	Tc
Bismuth	Bi	Helium	He	Oxygen	O	Tellurium	Te
Boron	B	Holmium	Ho	Palladium	Pd	Terbium	Tb
Bromine	Br	Hydrogen	H	Phosphorus	P	Thallium	Tl
Cadmium	Cd	Indium	In	Platinum	Pt	Thorium	Th
Calcium	Ca	Iodine	I	Plutonium	Pu	Thulium	Tm
Californium	Cf	Iridium	Ir	Polonium	Po	Tin	Sn
Carbon	C	Iron	Fe	Potassium	K	Titanium	Ti
Cerium	Ce	Krypton	Kr	Praseodymium	Pr	Tungsten	W
Cesium	Cs	Lanthanum	La	Promethium	Pm	Uranium	U
Chlorine	Cl	Lawrencium	Lw	Protactinium	Pa	Vanadium	V
Chromium	Cr	Lead	Pb	Radium	Ra	Xenon	Xe
Cobalt	Co	Lithium	Li	Radon	Rn	Ytterbium	Yb
Copper	Cu	Lutetium	Lu	Rhenium	Re	Yttrium	Y
Curium	Cm	Magnesium	Mg	Rhodium	Rh	Zinc	Zn
Dysprosium	Dy	Manganese	Mn	Rubidium	Rb	Zirconium	Zr
Einsteinium	E	Mendelevium	Mv	Ruthenium	Ru		

than writing out the whole name of the element. Chemists call the abbreviations *chemical symbols*. This name is inherited from alchemists who, as we learned, actually used symbols to refer to chemical elements.

Some abbreviations are simply the first letter, or first two letters, of the element's name; for example, *iodine* (I) or *nickel* (Ni). Other abbreviations are composed of the first letter and one other letter in the element's name; for

example, *chlorine* (Cl) or *platinum* (Pt). These are easy to understand, but you may have noticed some abbreviations that are not made up of the letters in the element's name; for example, *gold* (Au). Why is this so? Because the letters of these abbreviations come from the Latin names of the elements. There is one other element whose abbreviation may puzzle you. It is *tungsten*, whose abbreviation is *W*. This is so because the proper name of tungsten is *wolfram,* but it is a matter of custom to call this element tungsten in the United States. Here is a list of those elements whose abbreviations are derived from the Latin name:

ENGLISH NAME	LATIN NAME	ABBREVIATION
gold	*aurum*	Au
silver	*argentum*	Ag
copper	*cuprum*	Cu
iron	*ferrum*	Fe
lead	*plumbum*	Pb
tin	*stannum*	Sn
mercury	*hydrargyrum*	Hg
antimony	*stibnium*	Sb
potassium	*kalium*	K
sodium	*natrium*	Na

CHEMICAL COMPOUNDS

What are chemical compounds?

There are only 106 chemical elements, but we know of almost a million other materials. What are these materials? They are combinations of two or more chemical elements and are called *chemical compounds.* To *compound* means "to put together." Chemical compounds are made by putting together chemical elements.

There are many compounds familiar to you. Water is one. Salt is another. Vinegar, sugar, aspirin, chalk, epsom salts, gasoline, lime, marble, rouge, washing soda and alcohol are still other compounds you know. Most of the materials you handle or use are chemical compounds or mixtures of chemical compounds.

Let us see of what elements a few familiar chemical compounds are made. (As you read the following, you may want to refer to the table of chemical elements.) Water is made of the elements *hydrogen* and *oxygen.* Table salt is made of *sodium* and *chlorine.* Chalk is made up of *calcium, carbon* and *oxygen.* Rouge is a combination of *iron* and *oxygen.* Alcohol is composed of *carbon, hydrogen* and *oxygen.*

When we say that water is made up of the elements hydrogen and oxygen, do we mean that if we mix together some hydrogen and some oxygen, we will have some water? No, for in order to make a chemical compound, we usually must use very special means of combining chemical elements. For example, if we were to put some oxygen in a jar that we previously emptied of air, and then were to add twice as great a volume of hydrogen, we would not be able to tell the contents of the jar from air simply by looking. But if we put into the jar two wires connected to an electric battery, and made a spark jump between the ends of the wires, we would cause an explosion within the jar. And

Water is a compound of oxygen and hydrogen.

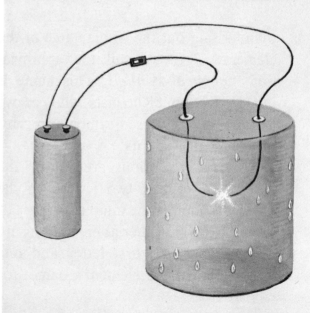

all around the sides of the jar would appear tiny drops of water. Since there was nothing at all in the jar until we put the hydrogen and oxygen into it, the water must have come from the combination of the two elements put into the jar. A chemist says that the hydrogen and oxygen *combined chemically* to form the compound called water.

An electric spark is not the only method of causing elements to combine into compounds; in fact, it is a rare method. One very common method is to heat the materials that we want to combine into compounds. Another method is to dissolve materials in water or other liquids, and then to mix the liquids, perhaps also heating them.

Since all compounds are made of elements, and since elements can be combined in so many different ways to make so many thousands of compounds, you can probably see the similarity between chemical elements and building blocks. It is because almost all the materials that we know of in the universe are made up of elements, compounds, or mixtures of these two, that elements are truly the building blocks of the universe.

Fill a tumbler half full of vinegar.

How can you make a compound?

Crush a small piece of chalk. (If some kinds of chalk don't work, use crushed egg shell.) Drop the chalk into the vinegar. Soon you will see bubbles rising from the chalk. Where did they come from? They are made of *carbon dioxide* gas. This gas is composed of the elements carbon and oxygen combined into a single compound — the carbon dioxide.

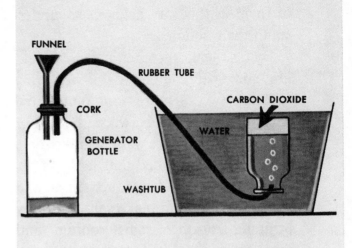

To make carbon dioxide, set up this apparatus. Place one-half inch of bicarbonate of soda in the generator bottle. Pour three ounces of vinegar into the funnel. To put the collection bottle in place, fill it with water, place your hand tightly over its mouth, turn it upside down under water, remove your hand.

The carbon and the oxygen, along with the element calcium, made up the chalk. The vinegar was able to remove the calcium from the chalk compound, leaving the carbon and oxygen to form the gas.

To combine two or three or more elements in order to make compounds is an unusual way of

In what other ways can we make compounds?

doing things in chemistry. Pure elements are difficult to obtain and are therefore expensive. Also, certain elements seem to be so eager to combine with others that it is difficult to keep them pure until we want to use them. Other elements seem so unwilling to combine that they require a great amount of trouble and expense to cause them to join with others. (Of course, chemical elements have no feelings, so they cannot really be "eager" or "unwilling," but to think of them in this way helps us to understand their actions.)

By far the most common way of making chemical compounds is to bring together two or more compounds and exchange elements between them. For example, suppose we want to make some table salt. We learned that table salt is made up of the elements sodium and chlorine. We could make salt by simply bringing together some sodium and some chlorine. But if we actually tried this, we would find that we had problems on our hands. Chlorine is a very poisonous green gas, so it is difficult and dangerous to handle. Sodium is a metal that combines very easily with the oxygen of the air so that we would have a hard time to keep it pure until we could bring it into contact with the chlorine. And then, even if we solved these problems, there would be another,

for when the chlorine and sodium were brought into contact, they would begin to combine so energetically that an explosion would result.

There is, however, a very neat way in which we can combine sodium and chlorine. We could obtain two inexpensive, easy-to-handle powdered compounds called calcium chloride and sodium carbonate. Calcium chloride is made up of the elements calcium and chlorine, and sodium carbonate is made up of the elements sodium, carbon and oxygen. Now, both these compounds can be dissolved in water without combining with the water. Having dissolved the calcium chloride and the sodium carbonate in separate containers of water, we pour the water from both containers together. What happens? Again speaking figuratively, the sodium rushes into the arms of the chlorine, and the

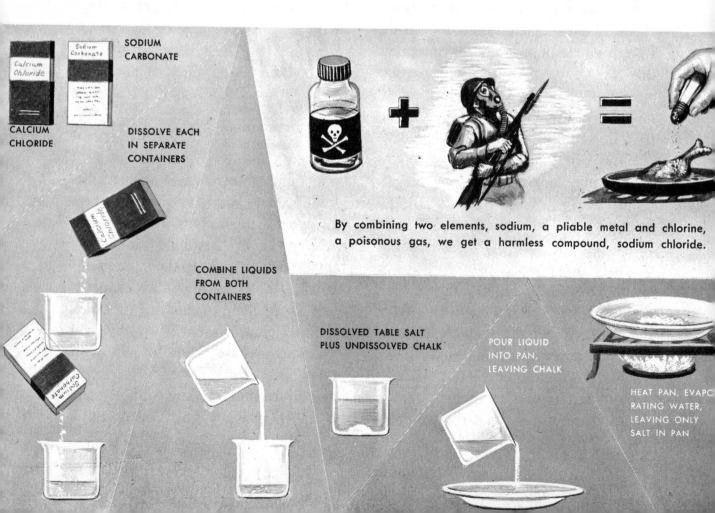

CALCIUM CHLORIDE

SODIUM CARBONATE

DISSOLVE EACH IN SEPARATE CONTAINERS

By combining two elements, sodium, a pliable metal and chlorine, a poisonous gas, we get a harmless compound, sodium chloride.

COMBINE LIQUIDS FROM BOTH CONTAINERS

DISSOLVED TABLE SALT PLUS UNDISSOLVED CHALK

POUR LIQUID INTO PAN, LEAVING CHALK

HEAT PAN, EVAPORATING WATER, LEAVING ONLY SALT IN PAN

calcium joins hands with the carbon and oxygen.

The sodium and chlorine have formed table salt, but what have the rest of the elements made? The leftover elements are calcium carbon and oxygen. You may remember we learned that chalk is made up of calcium, carbon and oxygen — and chalk is exactly what the rest of our elements have combined to make. This chalk is in the form of very, very fine particles.

Chalk will not dissolve in water. So, the tiny particles of chalk simply settle to the bottom of the container of water. Let us wait for all the chalk to settle. Then we very carefully pour the water (and the salt dissolved in it) into a pan, leaving the chalk behind. We heat the pan until all the water boils away, and left on the bottom of the pan is pure *sodium chloride*, or table salt.

ATOMS AND MOLECULES

All matter is made up of extremely small particles called *atoms*. Atoms are so small that no microscope, no matter how powerful, can enable you to see them. One hundred million atoms, side by side, would make a row only one inch long. We know of 103 kinds of atoms, each of a different size. Does the number *103* remind you of anything? You probably remember that there are 103 chemical elements. Each element is made up of just one kind of atom. We

What are atoms and molecules?

learned that an element is matter that cannot be divided into simpler parts. Now we can see that this is true because all of an element is made up of atoms of the same kind. No matter how much we divide up an element, we still have the same kind of atoms. (Of course, you may have heard of scientists who split, or smash, atoms. But when an atom is split, part of it becomes heat and light — and we learned that heat and light are not kinds of matter. So, we cannot properly say that splitting an atom divides it into simpler parts.)

We learned that elements are the simplest kinds of matter with which a chemist works. Now that we know what an atom is, we can add that an atom is the smallest unit of matter with which a chemist works.

Atoms sometimes exist by themselves, without connection to other atoms. Mostly, though, atoms form groups with other atoms. There may be only two atoms in a group or there may be hundreds. These groups of atoms are called *molecules*.

Sometimes two atoms of the same element join together to form a molecule. Chemists tell us that this two-atom molecule makes up most gases — hydrogen, oxygen and nitrogen, for example.

Usually, a molecule is made up of atoms of different elements. We learned that a chemical compound, too, is made up of different elements. Now, we can add that a compound is made up of molecules. When we learned that elements combine to make compounds, what we also meant was that atoms combine to make molecules.

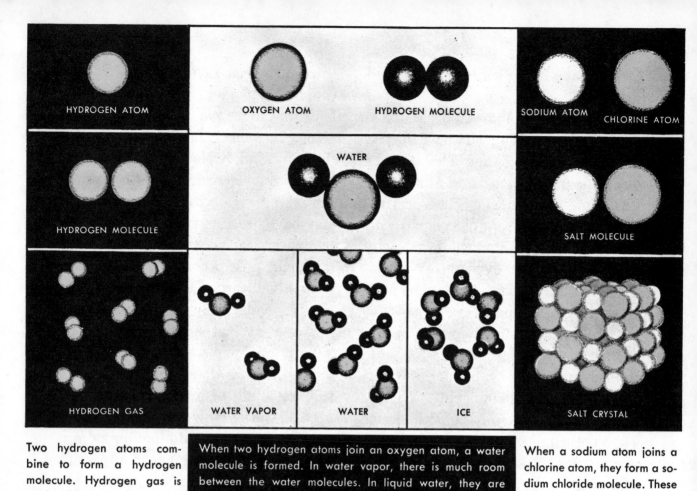

HYDROGEN ATOM   OXYGEN ATOM   HYDROGEN MOLECULE   SODIUM ATOM   CHLORINE ATOM

HYDROGEN MOLECULE   WATER   SALT MOLECULE

HYDROGEN GAS   WATER VAPOR   WATER   ICE   SALT CRYSTAL

Two hydrogen atoms combine to form a hydrogen molecule. Hydrogen gas is made of hydrogen molecules.

When two hydrogen atoms join an oxygen atom, a water molecule is formed. In water vapor, there is much room between the water molecules. In liquid water, they are closer together. In ice, they form shapely ice crystals.

When a sodium atom joins a chlorine atom, they form a sodium chloride molecule. These molecules join to form salt.

How do atoms combine?

You probably know that a magnet will attract a piece of iron or steel, and that two magnets will attract each other. Atoms act like tiny magnets. They attract each other and join together. Since there are 103 different kinds of atoms, there are a vast number of ways in which they can join together. This is why there are so many compounds.

Not only can atoms join in so many different combinations, but also in many different patterns. Let us see some of these patterns. Suppose you could enlarge atoms until they became as large as marbles. With these large atoms, you could make models of molecules.

You might place two atoms side by side to form a model of a gas molecule.

You might add a third atom so as to form a triangular molecule. This would be the model of a water molecule. The oxygen atom would be larger than the two hydrogen atoms joined to it. If you wanted to add a fourth atom, you would place it on top of the other three, so as to form a little pyramid. In this case, the atoms would all have to be nearly the same size.

You might join all your atoms in a single row. Certain atoms actually do join in long rows, or chains, as the chemist calls them. You might join your atoms in the form of a circle. There really are molecules that are in the form of circles, or rings, as the chemist calls them. We shall learn more about chains and rings, because these arrangements of atoms make molecules of the greatest importance to man.

MIXTURES

What is a mixture? We have been talking about mixtures of many kinds of materials. In chemistry, we must clearly understand what a mixture is, so let us make one. We take a handful of the element *iron* in the form of filings; that is, in the form of powdered iron. Then we take a handful of the element *sulfur,* also in the form of a fine powder. We put enough of the two handfuls into a bottle so that the bottle is only half full. We cap the bottle and roll it around and around. Doing this thoroughly mixes the particles of iron and sulfur.

Is the mixture the same as a compound made up of iron and sulfur? No, because there are two important differences. To understand what these differences are, let us try two experiments.

First, let us see whether we can think of a way to separate the particles of iron and sulfur that make up our mixture. We might get a very fine pair of tweezers and try to pick all the particles of iron out of the mixture, thus leaving the sulfur behind. The trouble with this idea is that we couldn't get a pair of tweezers fine enough, nor probably have enough patience to pick out every single piece of iron. There is, however, an easy way to separate the iron and sulfur. We simply pull a magnet back and forth through our mixture. The iron particles cling to the magnet — the sulfur particles do not. Thus, we can separate the iron and sulfur, and no longer have a mixture.

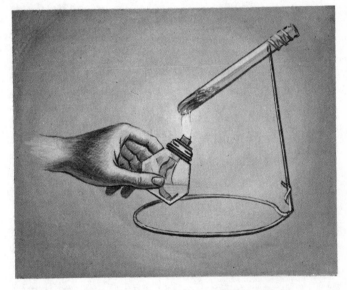

Sulphur and iron joined in a compound do change.

Sulphur and iron joined in a mixture stay unchanged.

Can we separate a compound of iron and sulfur in the same way? Let us see. We make the iron and sulfur mixture again. Now we put the mixture into a small porcelain crucible, or a test tube. We then heat the tube. At the proper temperature, the mixture begins to glow and give off heat, as if it were burning. When the glowing stops and the tube cools, let us dump out the contents and examine it closely.

21

Out of the tube comes a lump made up of black crystals. We no longer see particles of either iron or sulfur. If we bring a magnet close to the lump, nothing clings to the magnet. What happened to the particles of iron and sulfur that went into the mixture? They combined chemically to form the crystals that are a compound called *iron sulfide*. Can we separate iron sulfide into iron and sulfur? Yes, but doing so will be a long and complicated process in which we use many compounds and several chemical operations.

Now we can see what is the first difference between

How do mixtures and compounds differ?

a mixture and a compound: The materials that make up a mixture remain unchanged in the mixture; but the materials that go into making a compound change completely as they form the compound. We learned about a very dramatic change of this kind when we saw how two gases, hydrogen and oxygen, combine to form a liquid, water. There are thousands of solid compounds, part of whose ingredients are gases or liquids, and there are liquid compounds whose ingredients are solids or gases.

When we were making the mixture of iron filings and sulfur powder, we could have mixed together as much or as little of each of these ingredients as we wished. We could have used half iron and half sulfur or ten times as much of one as the other.

In making a compound we do not have a free choice of how much of each ingredient we will have in the compound. In iron sulfide there is combined just one part of iron with one part of sulfur — no more and no less. If we had used more iron than sulfur, the extra iron would have been left over. (We may not have been able to see the extra iron just by looking, but if we had ground up the lump of iron sulfide and then pulled a magnet through the powder, we could have removed the *extra* iron, but not the iron that combined with the sulfur to make iron sulfide.)

Now we know the second difference between a mixture and a compound: A mixture can be made up of ingredients in any amounts, but a compound is made up of ingredients in only certain fixed amounts that are always the same.

RAIN

FRESH WATER

OCEAN

There is one kind of mixture that does not act like other mixtures. Let us make it. First we take a glass of water into which we place a teaspoon of table salt. Stir the water with a spoon. What happens to the salt? It disappears. A chemist says that the salt *dissolves*. The water and the dissolved salt together make up a solution.

When is a mixture not a mixture?

Let us pour the solution from the glass into a pan and put the pan on a lighted stove. We let the solution boil until all of the water goes up in steam. On the bottom of the pan is the same amount of salt as we dissolved in the glassful of water.

Insofar as the solution can be made up of ingredients in varying amounts, it is like a mixture. Also, the ease with which we separated the ingredients shows that they were not chemically combined to form a compound. In this way, too, a solution is like a mixture. But when the salt was dissolved in the water, we could not see separate parts of salt and water, for the salt had taken on an entirely new form. In this way the solution is different from a mixture.

How is a solution and mixture alike and different, too?

There is more than one kind of solution. Not only can solids (like salt) be dissolved in liquids (like water), but liquids can be dissolved in other liquids, and gases can be dissolved in liquids. We have learned that the bubbles in soda water are carbon dioxide gas. We see bubbles only when the carbon dioxide begins to separate from the water in which it was dissolved.

Solutions are very important in chemistry. By dissolving materials — compounds and elements — in liquids, the chemist has his chief way of bringing materials together to form new

How do the chemists form new compounds?

CONDENSATION

EVAPORATION

SALT·WATER

Nature is continually manufacturing fresh and salt water. The sun's heat evaporates water from the sea to form clouds that are made up of fresh-water droplets. Rain from the clouds runs through the ground and dissolves salt compounds. Streams and rivers carry the dissolved salts to the sea where the salt collects, and the sea becomes saltier. The sun evaporates more sea water as the process continues.

23

compounds. Do you remember that when we were learning about compounds, we found how to make table salt (sodium chloride) from two other compounds called calcium chloride and sodium carbonate? These latter two were powdered. If we simply mixed the powders together, kept them dry and left them alone, nothing would have happened. But we dissolved the powders in water. Then the compounds easily acted to form new compounds. In the chemical industry, dissolving compounds in liquids is probably the main way of bringing materials together to make new materials.

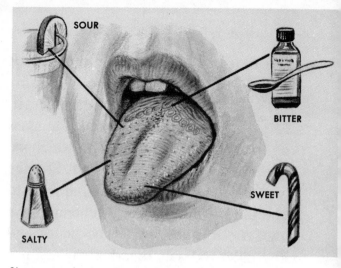

Shown are the location of taste buds on the tongue.

Solutions are important to us when we eat. Our tongues have

How do we taste things?

certain areas in which there are small organs called *taste buds*. Different taste buds give us different taste sensations. There are taste buds for sweet, sour, salty and bitter tastes. We do not know exactly how taste buds work, but we do know that tasting is some kind of chemical

action. How do we know this? Because we can taste only those materials that dissolve in liquids. Saliva is one liquid that dissolves some of our food materials; water is another.

If you want to prove that a material must be dissolved in order to be tasted, try to taste a clean spoon or the edge of a clean plate. Neither silver nor china can dissolve in your saliva. That is why you cannot taste either of them. Put a dry soda cracker in your mouth. At first, you will taste nothing. In a few seconds, your saliva will begin to dissolve the cracker, and you will taste it.

Some Interesting Elements

Each of the 103 chemical elements has an interesting story. Elements have different colors. Some are metals, some are crystals, some are liquids and some are gases. Elements are obtained in many different ways, and elements have many interesting uses. Let us look closely at a few of them.

We have learned that alchemists dis-

Which element is noted for glowing in the dark, and how was it found?

covered several chemical elements, but we know about the actual discovery of only one of these elements. In 1669, a German alchemist, Hennig Brand, was trying to make gold from cheaper materials. Because gold was considered to be the most perfect metal, alchemists called it a "noble" metal. Brand reasoned that nothing could be more noble than the human body and materials connected with it. So, perhaps, it would be possible to change something connected with the noble human body into the noble metal, gold.

With this idea in mind, Brand mixed together some human urine and sand, and heated them in an oven. We do not know why he chose sand, but it was not unusual for alchemists to heat together any odd combination of materials that came to mind. When taken from the cooled oven, Brand's mixture glowed strongly in the dark. Brand had not, of course, made gold, but he had made a soft, whitish, waxy material. This material had been in a compound dissolved in the urine, although Brand did not know this. He named the glowing material *phosphorus,* which is Greek for the words "I bear light." Phosphorus turned out to be an element — it could not be divided into simpler materials.

A century and a half after the discovery of this element, it was found that phosphorus mixed with other materials would catch fire when rubbed. This mixture was used to make tips for matches. Unfortunately, since phosphorus is very poisonous, many people who worked in match factories died from breathing the vapor of heated phosphorus. But fortunately, in 1845, another kind of phosphorus—red phosphorus—was discovered. It is not poisonous and eventually, all countries passed laws that

At the left is an alchemist's oven; right, Brand discovers phosphorus.

The English scientist Robert Boyle, in 1660, put a live mouse and a lighted candle into a sealed glass jar that was attached to a pump. He pumped the air out of the jar, and the candle went out and the mouse died. This proved to Boyle that he was right in believing that air contains a substance necessary to sustain life.

banned the use of white phosphorus in the manufacture of matches.

Phosphorus is very important to the **Why is phosphorus useful to humans?** proper growth of the human body, especially for the development of healthy bones and teeth. Phosphorus is also needed to keep nerves and muscles healthy. The phosphorus in our bodies is combined with other chemical elements and is not at all poisonous. We can get enough phosphorus for good health from a balanced diet, especially from milk. Plants, too, need phosphorus, and this element is a part of most fertilizers.

Sometimes chemists need large amounts of phosphorus. To get it, they put burned bones or a certain kind of rock, called phosphate rock, into a furnace along with sand and coke. In both the bones and rock there are compounds containing much phosphorus. This mixture is heated, and large amounts of phosphorus are obtained as a result of this process.

The most abundant element on earth **What is the most abundant element in the earth's crust?** is a colorless, odorless, tasteless gas that is important to you every moment of your life. This element is *oxygen*. One-fifth of the weight

The French chemist Antoine Lavoisier showed that when oxygen combines *slowly* with iron or certain other metals, rusting takes place, and when oxygen combines *rapidly* with the elements that make up wood, for example, burning occurs. This sort of rapid combining of oxygen with a substance is *combustion*.

In the year 1771 Joseph Priestley, the English scientist, prepared oxygen by concentrating the sun's rays through a lens on mercuric oxide.

of the atmosphere and nine-tenths of the weight of all the earth's water is oxygen. Nearly half of the weight of the earth's rocky crust and one-third of the weight of the deeper rocks is oxygen. And oxygen makes up two-thirds of your body and the tissues of most other living things.

In the late fifteenth century, the Italian scientist and artist Leonardo da Vinci wrote that the atmosphere contained two different gases. Two hundred years later, an Englishman, John Mayow, discovered that one of the gases in air caused iron to rust and was important to breathing. Sixty years later another Englishman, Stephen Hales, actually obtained some oxygen by heating a compound called saltpeter. Hales, like the alchemists, called all gases "air," and so he never knew he discovered a new gas. Exactly forty years later, a Swedish apothecary, Karl Wilhelm Scheele, produced some pure oxygen. He realized that he had discovered a new gas, but he did not have any way of telling the scientific world about it. Three years later, Joseph Priestley, an English clergyman, also produced pure oxygen. He immediately told his fellow scientists about his accomplishment. Scheele did not publish his results until three years after Priestley reported his discovery. For this reason, Priestley was for a long time given credit as the discoverer of oxygen, but now we say that both men deserve equal credit as the discoverers of this important element.

Oxygen is very useful in a chemical laboratory and also in industry. If we want just a little oxygen we have several ways of obtaining it. We might get oxygen the way Priestley did; that is, we could heat a compound called mercuric oxide. This compound is a reddish powder that is composed of the elements mercury and oxygen. Gently heating mercuric oxide will cause the oxygen to separate from the mercury. There are a few other compounds from which we could get oxygen by heating them.

How can we get oxygen?

Still another way to get small amounts of oxygen is to run an electric current through water. We learned that water is composed of hydrogen and oxygen. The electric current separates the atoms of the water molecule, and water changes into hydrogen and oxygen.

In industry, much larger amounts of oxygen are needed than can be conveniently obtained by the methods described above. To obtain large amounts of oxygen, we turn to the air, which is one-fifth oxygen. This portion of oxygen is not combined with any other element. To separate the oxygen from the eight other gases that normally make up the atmosphere, air is put into containers under very great pressure. As a result the air becomes liquid and very cold. Then the pressure is gradually released and the liquid air is allowed to slowly warm up. As the warming takes place, each of the gases that make up the air boils off at a different temperature. Oxygen boils off at 297 degrees below zero Fahrenheit. As the oxygen boils off it is caught in other containers, and then is stored in stout steel cylinders at a pressure of 2,000 pounds per square inch. The cylinders are shipped to laboratories or factories that use oxygen.

Did you ever think that there is a connection between a burning match and a rusting nail? Well, there is. When a match burns, oxygen is *rapidly* combining with some of the elements that make up the wood of the match. When a nail rusts, oxygen is *slowly* combining with the iron of the nail. In both these cases, the combining oxygen is producing heat. It is easy to tell that a burning match gives off heat; it is difficult to measure the heat given off by a rusting nail, but it can be done. This sort of combination of oxygen with other kinds of matter is called *combustion*.

How is oxygen used by the human body?

When you breathe air into your lungs, some of the air is taken into the blood and carried through the arteries to food materials stored in the muscles and other tissues. Here the oxygen combines with the food materials and produces heat to warm your body and energy to move your muscles. This combination of oxygen with the food materials is really slow combustion, just like the rusting of a nail. Since your heart must continue to beat as long as you are alive, you have a continuous need for energy; so you must continuously burn food materials in your tissues to keep your heart beating. When a human being is deprived of air for even a few minutes — as, for example, in drowning — his heart cannot get the oxygen it needs for energy, and the heart stops beating. Thus, oxygen is not only the most abundant element, but it is also the most important to living beings.

Everyone has seen some form of the element carbon. A piece **Why are diamonds so hard?** of coal, a burned match, the lead of a lead-pencil, a diamond, and soot from a burning candle — all these are forms of the element carbon. A diamond is the hardest natural material known. (Up until very recently, diamond was the hardest, but now chemists have made a compound of the elements carbon and boron that is harder than diamond.) A diamond is so hard because the carbon atoms that make up the diamond are packed very closely together.

Everyone knows that diamonds are valuable, and one that is entirely transparent, with no elements mixed into it to color it, is very rare. The closely-packed atoms of a diamond have a remarkable effect on light that passes through the diamond. They cause the light to come out of the diamond in bright sparkles of all the colors of the rainbow. Because of this, we say that a diamond has *fire* and *luster,* and these two qualities are what make diamonds so highly prized as jewels.

Some diamonds are black or dark brown. These diamonds are used in industry to cut, grind or drill hard metals, such as steel.

Until recently, all diamonds were mined from the earth. But in 1955, an American company began to manufacture diamonds. These diamonds are the black kind. The manufacturing process is a secret, but we can make a pretty

ROUGH DIAMONDS

CUT DIAMOND

THREE FORMS OF CARBON:
DIAMONDS
GRAPHITE
COAL

GRAPHITE

LIGNITE

ANTHRACITE

BITUMINOUS COAL

Charcoal is made out of wood.

During the "coal age," about 250 million years ago, huge tree-ferns and giant mosses flourished in the hot, humid weather. These plants toppled to the ground when they died and sank in the mud, forming the basis for coal deposits.

good guess at how it is done. In 1887, a French chemist named Henri Moissan dissolved some charcoal (a form of carbon) in molten iron. He plunged the iron into water. The cooling iron exerted tremendous pressure on the dissolved carbon, and the carbon formed tiny diamonds. The modern process, too, uses some kind of great pressure to squeeze the carbon atoms as close together as they are found in diamonds.

What causes the "writing" when you write with a lead pencil?

The lead in a lead pencil is not really made of the element lead — it is a form of carbon called *graphite*. (Once upon a time, lead pencils actually did have thin rods of lead in them.) The carbon atoms in graphite are connected together in the form of thin sheets. These sheets, layer upon layer, easily slide over one another. This is why part of the graphite of a pencil so easily slides off to leave a line on the paper upon which we are writing. Powdered graphite is used instead of oil to help parts of machines to slide easily over one another.

How is charcoal made?

In the third kind of carbon, represented by charcoal and carbon black, the atoms are arranged in tiny interlocking flakes. This is called *amorphous* carbon. Charcoal is made by burning wood in an insufficient supply of air. Carbon black is made by burning natural gas under like conditions. Burning in this manner gets rid of the other materials that make up wood and natural gas, and leaves behind nearly pure carbon.

Carbon black has many uses. You are looking at one of them right now.

30

Carbon black mixed with the proper oils makes printer's ink. Also, the ink on black typewriter ribbons and the surface of black carbon paper contain carbon black. Carbon black is added to rubber to increase its toughness and wearing qualities. Every automobile tire contains several pounds of carbon black.

Coal is almost all carbon. *Bituminous,* or soft, coal is eighty-eight percent carbon, while *anthracite,* or hard, coal is ninety-five percent carbon. You probably know that all coal is mined, but how did the coal happen to be in the ground? About 250 million years ago, the climate all over the world, except in the most northern parts, was warm and damp. It rained much, and it was always as warm as it

Where did coal come from? How was it formed?

now is in tropical regions. Swamps covered much of the surface of the earth. Among the many plants that grew in abundance in the warm, wet climate were some called tree-ferns. They looked like huge ferns, some being a hundred feet tall. There were no trees in the world at this time. The tree-ferns were not made of wood, but of a softer material. However, like wood, this material was largely carbon. The trunks of tree-ferns were green and scaly, and at their tops grew fronds like those on fern plants today.

Tree-ferns grew in great numbers, making forests in all parts of the world. The forests were so thick and the tree-ferns grew so close together that no sunlight could ever shine through the fern tops to the ground beneath.

When the tree-ferns died, they fell into the swamps in which they were standing and sank into the mud. More

The pressure of layers of tree-ferns and mud as well as the earth's folding crust changed plants to coal beds.

Thousands of compounds from vanilla flavoring and medicine to perfume and explosives are made out of coal tar by chemists.

tree-ferns died and fell upon those that were already buried. More mud covered the newly-fallen plants. The weight of the fallen tree-ferns and the mud pressed heavily upon those that were buried deeply. Water and other liquids were pressed out of the tree-fern trunks. Later, tremendous pressure of the earth's folding crust further squeezed the remains of the buried plants. This process took tens of millions of years, and at its end, practically nothing was left of the buried tree-ferns but large masses of carbon. These masses are the coal beds that we mine for coal today.

Coal has been found in thirty-seven of the fifty United States. Last year, more than 600 million tons were mined. Most of this coal was burned to provide heat for homes and power for factories. Some of it was converted to methane gas through a process called *gasification*. Some was changed to a liquid by means of *liquefaction;* this also produced important by-products such as gasoline and fertilizer. About one-quarter of all the coal mined was used to make thousands of different kinds of plastics, dyes, varnishes and lacquers, perfumes, synthetic rubber, explosives and drugs.

How are several useful materials obtained from coal?

To obtain material from coal to make all the things we have just listed, the coal is placed into large ovens, called by-product ovens, from which all air is excluded. The coal is then heated red-hot. Ordinarily, at this heat, coal burns, but the coal in these ovens cannot burn. Since air is excluded from the by-product ovens, there is no oxygen to combine with the coal. Instead of burning, the heated coal separates into the materials from which it is made. Chief among these are coal gas, tar, coke, and a compound called ammonium sulfate. The coal gas may be piped away from the by-product ovens and sold to consumers for heating their homes or cooking their food. The ammonium sulfate is used to make fertilizer. Coke is used by iron and steel mills in smelting.

By separating coal tar into its principal compounds — benzene, toluene, phenol, anthracene and naphthalene — the chemist can make thousands of compounds ranging from vanilla flavoring and medicine to perfume and TNT.

If it had not been for *iron,* we would never have been able to build the great industries that have made modern civilization possible. Iron's strength, hardness and springy tough-

What is the most important element in modern times?

DOUBLE BELL
AND HOPPER

HOT GASES
TO BLAST
STOVES

IRON ORE,
COKE
AND LIME

PIPE FOR
HOT AIR
BLAST

MOLTEN
SLAG
AND
IRON

SLAG
OUTLET

IRON
OUTLET

The Bessemer process for converting pig iron into steel takes about fifteen minutes.

Metal is separated from ore in blast furnaces.

33

ness have made possible the construction of skyscraper frames, ocean liners, battleships, railroads, automobiles, typewriters, tanks and most of the machines and machine tools that have given us our industrial civilization.

In 4000 B.C., Egyptian pharaohs valued iron more highly than gold. At that time, the only iron available came from rare pieces that fell to earth as meteorites. It was not until 1500 B.C. that anyone learned to produce iron in fairly large quantities. At this time, a people of Asia Minor, the Hittites, learned how to obtain iron from iron ore. They used the iron to make swords, spears, helmets and shields. With these weapons they were very successful in war, because their enemies had bronze weapons that were softer than iron. Almost a thousand years more passed before most of the peoples who lived on the shore of the Mediterranean Sea had learned to obtain and use iron. When Julius Caesar landed in Britain, in 55 B.C., he found the people making iron.

Iron is the fourth most abundant element in the earth's crust, where it makes up one-twentieth of the total of all elements. However, if many scientists are correct in their belief that the earth's core (about 4,300 miles in diameter) is largely iron, then iron, and not oxygen, is the earth's most abundant element.

In the earth's crust, iron is in the form of iron ore. This

How do we put iron in a form so that it can be used by man? ore consists of iron combined with oxygen. In order to get the iron in a form we can use, we must

separate it from the oxygen. The process of doing this is called *smelting*. In general, smelting is done by heating iron ore mixed with charcoal or coke. Charcoal and coke both are forms of the chemical element, carbon. When iron ore and carbon are very hot, the atoms of oxygen become disconnected from the iron and connect with the carbon. This leaves iron in the form of the metal that is so familiar to us. What makes this process so easily workable is due to the fact that when the oxygen combines with the carbon, the compound that is formed is a gas that is driven off by the heat into the atmosphere. Thus, we do not have to worry about separating the carbon-and-oxygen compound from the iron we have obtained.

In the iron industry, smelting is done in huge ovens called *blast furnaces*. These furnaces are tall steel cylinders lined with brick, ten or twelve stories high. A fire is built in the bottom of the blast furnace, and iron ore and coke are dumped into the top of the furnace. At the bottom, encircling the furnace, is a ring of pipes. Through these pipes a strong blast of air is continually blown into the furnace in order to make the fire inside very hot. It is this blast of air that gives the blast furnace its name. In iron smelting plants, eight or ten blast furnaces are built next to each other in a double row. During the day, great columns of smoke pour out of the tops of the furnaces, while at night their fires light up the sky with a red glow.

The smelted iron collects at the bottom of the furnace. The iron is molten and runs as easily as water. When enough iron has collected, a hole is opened on the side at the bottom of the furnace. From this hole, the molten iron flows out of the furnace in a fiery stream. The iron flows into molds lined with sand. When the iron has cooled, it is in the shape of long heavy bars called "pigs," and the iron is thus called "pig iron." Most blast furnaces produce 400 to 500 tons of iron a day, and some can produce as much as 1,000 tons.

Pig iron is hard and strong, but it is brittle, which means that it is easily broken by a blow. If our machines were made of pig iron, we would continually have to be repairing their broken parts. What we need is a kind of iron that is tough as well as hard. The two main kinds of tough iron are called *wrought iron* and *steel*.

How is steel made?

If we add just the right amount of carbon to iron, we get steel. This kind of iron is not only tough, but it can be made very hard. Steel is easily shaped by casting, rolling, drawing and hammering. It has great resistance to breaking under pull. An excellent grade of steel was manufactured at Damascus and at Toledo in Spain during the Middle Ages. Swords manufactured in these two cities were highly prized for the springiness and hardness of the steel. The point of one of these swords could be bent all the way around to the hilt without breaking the blade. Armor, too, was made of steel.

One process for making steel uses a furnace called a *Bessemer converter*. It converts iron to steel, and was invented by Henry Bessemer. This furnace is a pear-shaped vessel, twelve to fifteen feet high, constructed of iron plates and lined with brick. It is hung by two thick, hollow iron rods attached to its sides at half its height, so that it can be tipped on its side. The brick lining is heated white-hot by a coal or oil fire. The converter is turned on its side and ten to twenty-five tons of molten pig iron are poured into it. It is brought back to an upright position and 20,000 cubic feet of air per minute are forced through one of the hollow supporting rods. The air enters the converter through the bottom and rushes upward through the molten iron. This burns out the impurities in the iron. The action is spectacular as a great torch of flame shoots out of the mouth of the converter with a roar and a shower of sparks. Within ten to twenty minutes the flame dies out. The converter is again turned on its side and a mixture

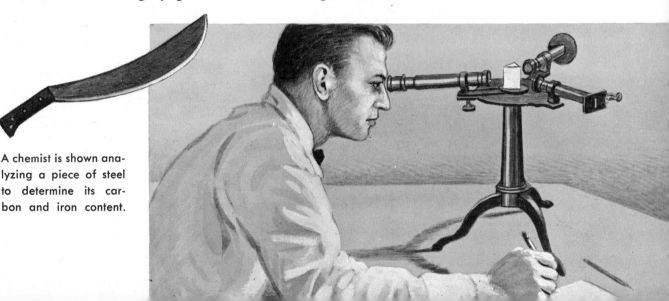

A chemist is shown analyzing a piece of steel to determine its carbon and iron content.

of the elements manganese and carbon is put into the converter. This mixture, called *spiegeleisen*, changes the iron to steel. A modern converter can produce one hundred tons of steel in an hour.

A modern steel and iron plant employs many chemists to analyze samples of steel and iron taken from the furnaces. In this way the steel and iron can be made to have the proper purity and other needed qualities.

Organic Chemistry

In the year 1828, a young German chemist, Friedrich Wöhler, made in his laboratory a compound called *urea*. The news of this accomplishment astounded the scientific world. Urea had been known as a compound made by human kidneys and as one of the waste products of the body. What, then, was so remarkable about Wöhler's making urea in a labo-

What is organic chemistry and carbon chemistry?

The German chemist Friedrich Wöhler, in 1828, accidentally made the organic compound urea in his laboratory. Wöhler's experiment destroyed the belief that compounds usually found in living things could not be made from non-living materials.

ratory? Before Wöhler's accomplishment, it had been believed that any of the materials of a living thing — plant or animal — or any of the products of these living things, contained an ingredient called a "vital spirit." This vital spirit was believed to be forever beyond man's grasp, and without it he could never reproduce any of the materials of which living things are made. By making urea in a laboratory, Wöhler had, at one stroke, destroyed the vital spirit theory.

As soon as the meaning of Wöhler's success was understood, scientists realized that the whole great field of the chemistry of living things had been opened. This new field of chemistry soon had two names: *organic chemistry* and *carbon chemistry*.

Since this field of chemistry had to do with the chemistry of living things — that is, living *organisms* — it is not hard to see where the name "organic chemistry" came from.

As knowledge of the field of organic chemistry grew, it was found that almost all of the tens of thousands of compounds found in living organisms not only contained carbon, but also depended on the properties of carbon. So the new field was also called *carbon chemistry*.

Since Wöhler's discovery, organic chemists have

How did a dream solve an important chemical problem?

studied more than 700,000 carbon compounds. It is now clear that carbon can form more compounds than any other element. Why? Because carbon

Carbon compounds: rubber, cotton, wood, sugar, wool.

atoms can connect to each other in long chains and in rings. Most molecules have only a few atoms, but carbon atom chains may contain hundreds of atoms. Usually, organic compounds contain hundreds of atoms. Carbon can combine with most other elements. There are more carbon compounds than all other chemical compounds put together. Wood, paper, wool, nylon, rubber, oil, alcohol, soap, fat and plastics are carbon compounds or mixtures of carbon compounds. Many compounds, called *hydrocarbons,* are composed only of carbon and hydrogen. Among them are natural gas, fuel oil, gasoline and paraffin. Other compounds, made up of carbon, hydrogen and oxygen, are called *carbohydrates*.

In working with these compounds, the organic chemist takes apart linkings of carbon chains and puts them together in different combinations. To understand what the organic chemist is

37

doing, you might picture a carbon atom as a tiny ball with four sharp hooks projecting from it at opposite points. These hooks can link up with the hooks on other carbon atoms or the atoms of other elements — hydrogen, for example. To understand just how carbon atoms are linked to each other or to other atoms requires many years of study by the organic chemist. Today, most chemists are organic chemists.

We learned that one way in which carbon atoms can link up is in rings. In the early days of organic chemistry, it was found that a large number of hydrocarbons had six carbon atoms joined in a ring. Organic chemists soon found they had a difficult problem when

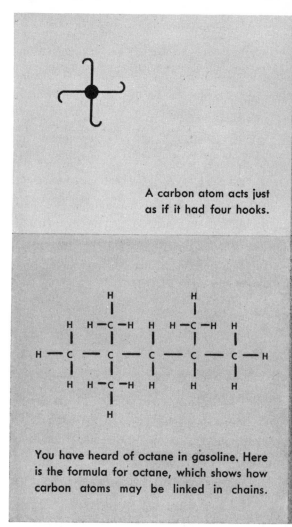

A carbon atom acts just as if it had four hooks.

You have heard of octane in gasoline. Here is the formula for octane, which shows how carbon atoms may be linked in chains.

Kekulé's dream solved the carbon ring linkage riddle.

they tried to figure out just how the carbon atoms formed the ring. Two of the connecting "hooks" on each carbon atom were used in joining it to the carbon atoms on each side of it. One more "hook" on each carbon atom was used to join some other atom to the ring, perhaps a hydrogen atom. But what was done with the other "hook"? If chemists considered it to be connected in a double connection to neighboring carbon atoms, they ended up with too many connections. They could not just consider it to be waving around empty, because all the "hooks" on an atom in a compound must be connected.

One afternoon, a German chemist, Friedrich Kekulé, who was working on the problem of the carbon ring linkage,

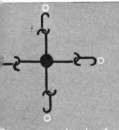

...bon atom hooks four ...gen atoms to form the ...c compound, methane.

...n can hook onto other ...ns as shown by the ...cal formula for ether.

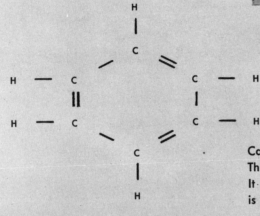

Since a carbon atom doesn't really have hooks, a chemist shows that a carbon atom can combine with four other atoms in the way shown here.

A chemist writes the formula for methane gas in this way.

Carbon atoms can link together in rings, too. This is the arrangement that Kekulé dreamed. It is the formula for benzene, a liquid that is used to dissolve varnishes and shellacs.

dozed off in a chair before the fireplace. Kekulé dreamed that he saw the six carbon atoms dancing around among the flames in his fireplace. Suddenly, the dancing atoms formed a ring with every "hook" used in just the right way. Kekulé remembered his dream when he awoke, and the problem of the six-atom ring was solved. The arrangement Kekulé dreamed is shown on this page.

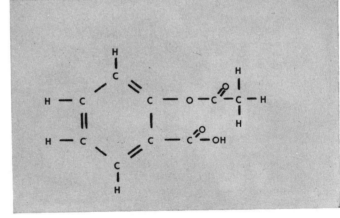

Here you can see carbon combining in many ways. The chemical formula shown above is for aspirin.

There is an old saying that all flesh is grass. This means

What do plants provide us with?

that all animals get their flesh either by eating plants or by eating other animals that eat plants. Cows and sheep eat grass. In their bodies, the grass eventually becomes flesh. Cougars do not eat grass,

but they do eat cows and sheep. In the body of the cougar, the cow and sheep flesh becomes cougar flesh. Thus, indirectly, cougar flesh comes from grass. Aphids eat the juices of rosebushes. Praying mantises eat aphids. Robins eat praying mantises. Hawks eat rob-

"FLESH IS GRASS"

CAT EATS BIRD,
THAT FEEDS ON INSECTS,
WHICH LIVE ON PLANTS.

bins. Thus, hawk flesh was once rose-bush juice. Human beings maintain the flesh on their bodies by eating both animal flesh and plants. In short, then, every animal is dependent on plants for food.

STOMATA

Leaves "inhale" carbon dioxide and "exhale" oxygen through small holes called *stomata*, shown above in a highly magnified cross section of a leaf. All green plants manufacture their own food in a process which scientists call *photosynthesis*.

Most plants — the green plants — manufacture their own food in a wonderful chemical factory. The green plant uses two raw materials: water from the soil and carbon dioxide gas from the air. To do the work of changing these two raw materials into food, the green plant needs energy — just as any chemical factory needs energy. The plant gets the needed energy from sunlight.

Where do plants get their food?

What kind of food does a green plant make from carbon dioxide and water? It makes a kind of sugar called *glucose*. If you were to eat some glucose you would find that it does not taste as sweet as the sugar you put on your cereal.

Right after a plant makes glucose in its leaves, the plant changes the glucose to starch. The starch, which is dissolved in water, is carried by the plant through tiny tubes in its stem to the root where the starch is stored.

In addition to making starch, a green plant makes *cellulose*, the main constituent of wood. Why is it that only green plants can make glucose, starch and cellulose? Because only green plants contain a carbon compound called *chlorophyll*. In fact, it is the green color of chlorophyll that makes plants green. The process in which a green plant uses water, carbon dioxide and chlorophyll to make glucose in the presence of sunlight is called *photosynthesis*. This word means "put together with the help of light."

1

2

3

Pin a strip of tinfoil or black cloth across the upper surface of some leaves of a house plant. A geranium is a good plant to use. Have each strip cover about a third of the leaf. Place the plant in a sunny window for two or three days. Cut the partly-covered leaves from the plant. Remove the tinfoil or cloth. Soak the leaves overnight in alcohol. The next day, take the leaves out of the alcohol. With a medicine dropper, drop iodine on both parts of the leaves that were covered and the parts that were not. The parts that were not covered will turn purple or dark blue. This color proves that starch is present.

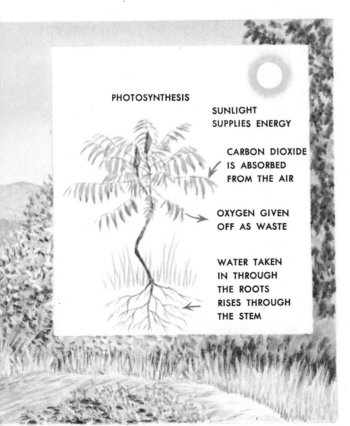

PHOTOSYNTHESIS

SUNLIGHT SUPPLIES ENERGY

CARBON DIOXIDE IS ABSORBED FROM THE AIR

OXYGEN GIVEN OFF AS WASTE

WATER TAKEN IN THROUGH THE ROOTS RISES THROUGH THE STEM

Chlorophyll plays a very interesting role in the process of photosynthesis. In a green plant, six molecules of carbon dioxide combine with six molecules of water and 673,000 calories of energy from sunlight to make one molecule of glucose and six molecules of oxygen. If the chlorophyll is not present, the sunlight will not cause the water and carbon dioxide to combine. Yet the chlorophyll does not become part of the glucose. Evidently, then, the chlorophyll helps the water and carbon dioxide become glucose, but the chlorophyll itself remains unchanged. Chemists know about many compounds that act this way. Such compounds are called *catalysts*. This term comes from the Greek words which mean "entirely loose" and refers to the fact that the catalyst is entirely loose from the compounds it helps to combine.

Chlorophyll: What does it do?

The chemical factory within a plant does not end its work with the making of glucose, starch and cellulose. The water that enters the plant through the roots brings with it many dissolved chemical compounds called *minerals*. The plant combines these minerals with starch to make fats, oils and proteins. You have probably noticed how oily peanuts are. Lima beans and kidney beans contain much protein. And nuts contain fat.

Did you ever stop to wonder why, during all the millions of years that animals have been living on earth, all the oxygen in the air was not long ago all breathed up? We just learned the answer to this question when we learned that the process of photosynthesis not only results in the manufacture of glucose, but also oxygen. So, it is the activity of plants that continually renews the oxygen in the air. But this is not the end of this wonderful arrangement. We learned that we slowly burn food materials in our tissues. These stored food materials are carbon compounds. When oxygen combines with these compounds, water and carbon dioxide gas are formed. When we exhale a breath from our lungs, it is made up partly of water and carbon dioxide. By breathing out carbon dioxide into the air, we make this gas available to plants for the process of photosynthesis.

What is the oxygen-carbon dioxide cycle?

Here we have a remarkable circular

HOW CAN YOU USE A CATALYST?

Place a lump of sugar in a saucer. Try to light it with a match. Can you make the sugar catch fire? No. Now rub the lump of sugar in an ashtray, so that the sugar picks up some cigarette or cigar ashes. Place a lighted match against the sugar where it is smeared with ash. Does it catch fire now? Answer: Yes. Did the ash act as a catalyst? Answer: Yes.

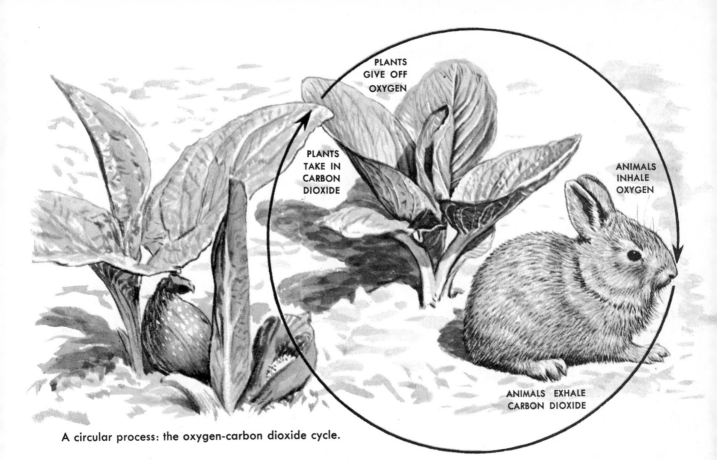

PLANTS
GIVE OFF
OXYGEN

PLANTS
TAKE IN
CARBON
DIOXIDE

ANIMALS
INHALE
OXYGEN

ANIMALS EXHALE
CARBON DIOXIDE

A circular process: the oxygen-carbon dioxide cycle.

arrangement: animals use oxygen and make carbon dioxide, while plants use that carbon dioxide and make oxygen for animals to use. The circular process is called the *oxygen-carbon dioxide cycle*. A cycle is a process that repeats itself over and over again.

How can you show that plants manufacture oxygen?

From a pond or stream get a plant that lives under water. The plants that are put into aquariums can also be used. Put the plant into a large jar or an aquarium full of water. Place the jar in a sunny window. Place a large glass funnel upside down over the plant. Fill a test tube with water. Keep your finger over the end of the test tube so that you do not lose any water from it, and then place the test tube upside down over the part of the funnel that is uppermost in the jar.

After two or three days of sunlight, you will see gas in the upper part of the test tube. You may also see gas bubbles sticking to the upper surfaces of the leaves of the plant. This gas is oxygen.

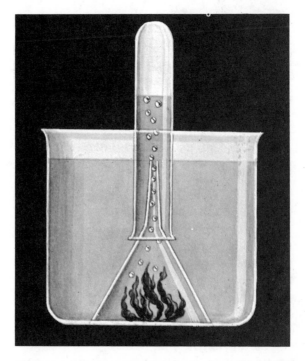

This experiment proves that plants give off oxygen.

43

Most chemists specialize in not more than one or two fields. Thousands are employed in the pharmaceutical industry, developing new drugs and cosmetics for a world market.

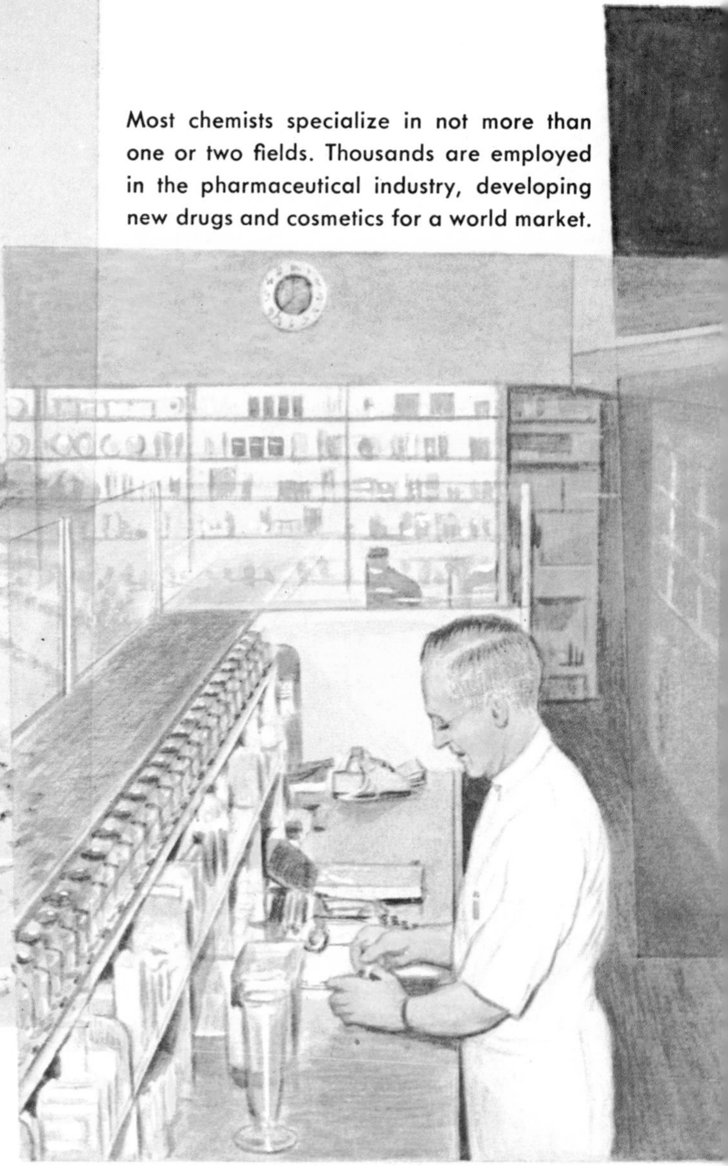

The agricultural chemist plays an important role in the development of new fertilizers and insecticides. Shown here is an airplane "dusting" cultivated land with insecticide.

The Branches of Chemistry

Chemistry is divided into several branches. Let us now explore some of them.

Man has been using chemistry in farm-

What is agricultural and food chemistry?

ing for a long time without knowing it. As far back as the Middle Ages, farmers used to leave one field out of three idle each year. They did not know the scientific reason why this was a good idea,

but they did know that after a field had lain idle for a year, it grew better crops. Modern *agricultural chemists* know that growing plants remove certain compounds from the soil. During the year that a field is left idle, the soil gets back from the air and from ground water the compounds that the plants removed. The next year, plants will then be able to obtain from this field the compounds they need. Thanks to agricultural chemists, we know what com-

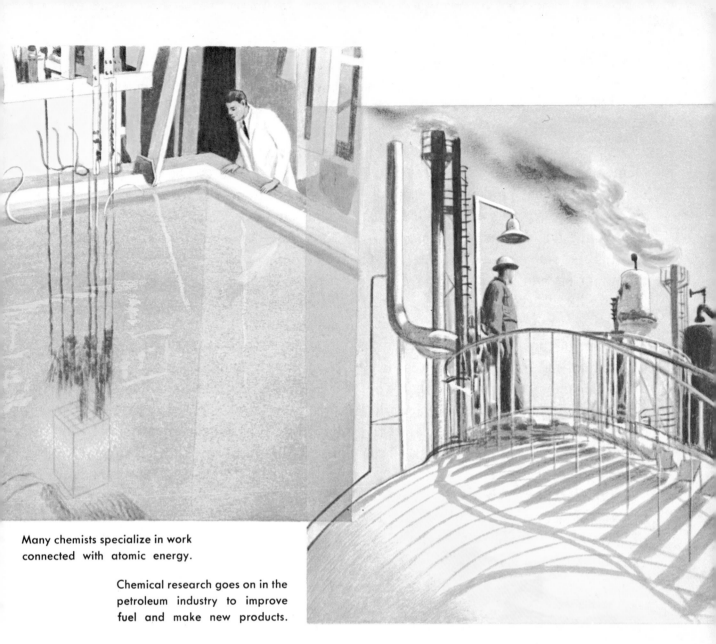

Many chemists specialize in work connected with atomic energy.

Chemical research goes on in the petroleum industry to improve fuel and make new products.

pounds plants need, and we put these compounds in the soil in the form of fertilizers. We no longer need to leave a field idle for a year.

Insects destroy millions of tons of food crops each year. This is a serious loss, but the amount of food insects would destroy if man did not fight them would be disastrous, probably causing starvation. It is the agricultural chemists who discover the sprays farmers must use to kill insects.

Once upon a time, well-fed cows in one part of the country were thin and sickly, while well-fed cows in other parts were fat and healthy. *Food chemists* learned that the healthy cows were fed corn that had the husks on the corn ears, but the sickly cows were fed wheat that had lost the wheat leaves during threshing. The husks are the leaves of the corn, and they have certain compounds cows need for health. When the sickly cows were fed green leaves, they too became healthy.

Food chemists are working on the possibility of making food for man from seaweed. As the population of the world increases, we soon may turn to the seas for other kinds of food besides fish.

We learned what organic chemistry is

What is inorganic chemistry? — the chemistry of carbon compounds. *Inorganic chemistry* includes the chemistry of all the other elements. One interesting group of compounds that modern inorganic chemists are working on is called *silicones*. The main element in these compounds is *silicon,* the second most abundant element in the earth's crust. Silicon, like carbon, can make compounds in the form of long chains. There are silicones that are rubbery and which won't crack in sub-zero weather. Other silicones are lubricants that will run in sub-zero weather. From these silicones are made gaskets, shock absorbers and other parts of machines that are used in polar regions.

Inorganic chemists have succeeded in producing compounds of krypton, radon, and xenon. These three elements (as well as helium, neon and argon) are known as *inert* gases, which means that they do not react readily with other chemicals. Until recently, it was not thought possible for such gases to form a compound.

We have learned that the slow burning

What is biochemistry? of food materials in the tissues of the human body is a kind of chemical change. This is not the only chemical change that goes on in the body. On the contrary, in every part of the body chemical changes are constantly taking place. One group of chemists, the *biochemists,* have studied the chemistry of the body. They have found so many hundreds of complicated chemical changes in the human body that they are still at the beginning of their study. From thousands of experiments they have gained revealing insights into body chemistry. The digestion of food, the changing of digested food into body tissue, the use of stored food, and the elimination of waste products — these are all activities that involve chemical changes. Biochemists have learned how the chemicals of the blood react with oxygen to form a protective scab on cuts that prevents the life fluid from draining way. And, more recently, they have been learning more about how chemicals such as deoxyribonucleic acid (DNA) and ribonucleic acid (RNA) affect heredity.

Medical chemistry is really a branch

What is medical chemistry? of biochemistry, but medical chemistry concerns itself with the diseases of the body. Did you ever hear of anyone being told by his doctor to take a laboratory test of his blood or urine? The blood is the transportation division of the body. Chemi-

CHEMISTRY AS A HOBBY

CHEMISTRY IN COOKING

CHEMISTRY IN RESEARCH

cal compounds dissolved in the blood are constantly being carried from one part of the body to another. The urine carries some of the body's waste compounds. Medical chemists have learned pretty well what compounds should be carried in the blood and urine of a healthy person. If medical chemists make tests on the blood and urine and find too much or too little of certain compounds, or if they find new compounds in these two body liquids, they can tell a doctor which of the organs of the body are not working properly.

In our bodies are certain organs called *glands*. These glands make chemical compounds that are put into the body's blood stream. For instance, one of these glands is the *adrenal gland*. It makes a compound called *adrenalin*. This compound makes our hearts beat faster when we are frightened or angry or excited. If you were to inject some adrenalin into a rabbit, you could make the rabbit so ferocious that it would attack and fight a dog. Medical biochemists discovered adrenalin and the compounds made by our glands.

Every day, doctors lean heavily on the work of medical chemists. In many cases, diagnoses which were almost impossible a few years ago are now quick and sure, thanks to the knowledge of the chemical processes of the body painstakingly gathered by medical chemists.

Is there still a need for new chemists today?

Although chemistry had its beginning thousands of years ago in the work of the first alchemists, chemistry is really a young science. Consider simply the fact that organic chemists have discovered more than 300,000 carbon compounds. Does this mean that most carbon compounds have been discovered and that it is becoming harder and harder to discover a new compound? No, it is quite the contrary. Since "discovering" new chemical compounds actually means making them by combining already-known compounds in new ways, the more compounds that are discovered, the more material there is to work with to make new compounds. It is for this reason that almost every day some new chemical discovery is announced. It may be a new man-made fiber with properties that neither cotton, wool, flax nor silk can match. It may be a new drug that will cure one of the diseases that are now considered to be incurable.

In agriculture there is a continuing need for chemists to find new ways of fighting the diseases and insects that destroy so much of our food crops. As

There is still a great need today for chemists in Federal Government work, in private industry and in schools. Whether you enjoy chemistry as a professional pursuit or as a hobby, it is a fascinating subject to follow.

Less than 200 years ago, Henry Cavendish isolated hydrogen by pouring acids over metals. He called the resulting gas "inflammable gas." Now, scientists have developed the most powerful explosive force known, the H-bomb. But it is within man's power to use the progress in chemistry to destroy life, or to enrich it.

planetary space. If it had not been for chemists who developed powerful rocket fuels, the first artificial satellite could not have been launched. Still more powerful rocket fuels are needed, and so are new compounds that will help rockets to better resist the great heat caused by their re-entry into the earth's atmosphere.

There is, too, a great need for teachers of chemistry — in public schools and colleges — who are not only able to teach their students how to combine atoms and molecules into new compounds according to the laws of chemistry, but who are also able to inspire their students to use science for the good of mankind. Endless opportunities await the chemist to help make the world a more comfortable and more humane place in which to live. This is the noble purpose of chemistry.

the population of the world increases so rapidly, chemists are wondering whether it might not be possible for man to make and use chlorophyll to produce food directly from the very abundant raw materials, water and carbon dioxide. This would do away with the need to grow crops, only part of which are used for food.

Man has just begun to explore inter-

48

THE HOW AND WHY WONDER BOOK OF
The HUMAN BODY

Written by MARTIN KEEN
Illustrated by DARRELL SWEET
Editorial Production: DONALD D. WOLF

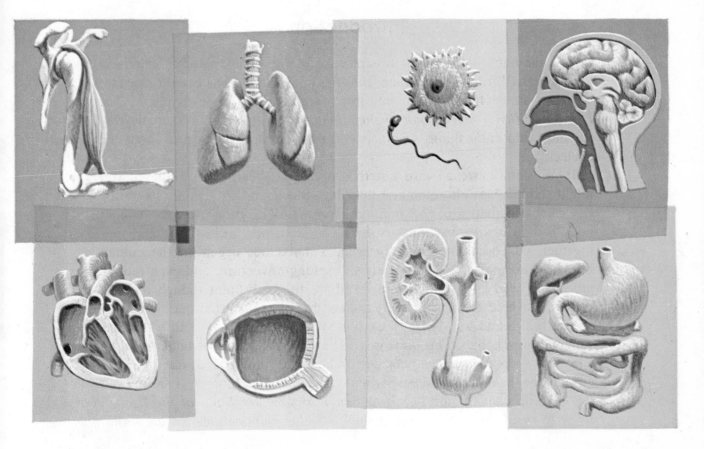

Edited under the supervision of
   Dr. Paul E. Blackwood
   Washington, D. C.

Text and illustrations approved by
   Oakes A. White, Brooklyn Children's Museum, Brooklyn, New York

GROSSET & DUNLAP • Publishers • NEW YORK

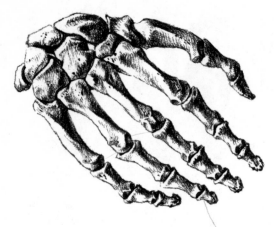

Introduction

It is the habit of scientists to explore, describe and explain all things in the universe. Little wonder, then, that the human body has been a constant object of study, for it is not only important but very close to home! *The How and Why Wonder Book of the Human Body* tells in a systematic way the most important things scientists and physicians have learned about the subject.

If you simply listened with a stethoscope to the beating of the heart, you might think it was an automatic machine. But if you could tune in on the remarkable activities of the brain cells, you would know that the human body is more than a machine. And as you learn how all the systems work together, you become amazed at what a marvelous organism the human body is. This makes the study of it an exciting adventure, and even though much has been known for centuries about the body, and though more is being discovered every year, there are still many unanswered questions.

The health and well-being of each of us depends on how well we understand our own bodies. This book is written to help us gain that understanding and may encourage many persons to choose a career of service in maintaining the health of others, perhaps as a nurse or doctor. Parents and schools will want to add *The How and Why Wonder Book of the Human Body* to their children's growing shelf of other publications in this series.

Paul E. Blackwood

Dr. Blackwood is a professional employee in the U. S. Office of Education. This book was edited by him in his private capacity and no official support or endorsement by the Office of Education is intended or should be inferred.

Library of Congress Catalog Card Number: 61-16034

ISBN: 0-448-05013-7 (WONDER EDITION)
ISBN: 0-448-04014-8 (TRADE EDITION)
ISBN: 0-448-03819-6 (LIBRARY EDITION)
1983 PRINTING

Copyright © 1961, 1969 by Grosset & Dunlap, Inc.
All rights reserved under International and Pan-American Copyright Conventions.
Published simultaneously in Canada.   Printed in the United States of America.

Contents

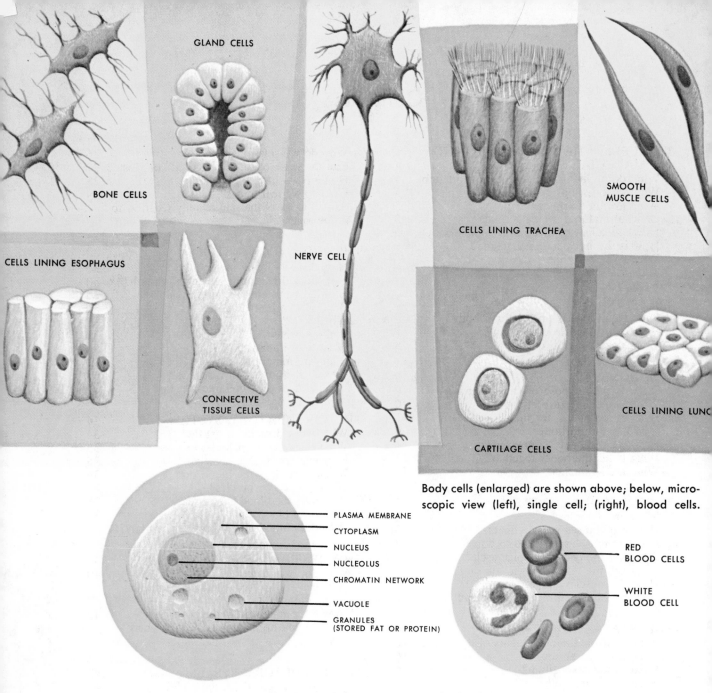

GLAND CELLS

BONE CELLS

CELLS LINING ESOPHAGUS

NERVE CELL

CONNECTIVE TISSUE CELLS

CELLS LINING TRACHEA

SMOOTH MUSCLE CELLS

CARTILAGE CELLS

CELLS LINING LUNG

Body cells (enlarged) are shown above; below, microscopic view (left), single cell; (right), blood cells.

PLASMA MEMBRANE
CYTOPLASM
NUCLEUS
NUCLEOLUS
CHROMATIN NETWORK
VACUOLE
GRANULES
(STORED FAT OR PROTEIN)

RED BLOOD CELLS

WHITE BLOOD CELL

The Cell, the Body's Building Material

Perhaps at some time you have visited a zoo. There you saw huge elephants, tall giraffes, comical little monkeys, strange birds and many other kinds of animals. The animals in the different cages were so different that you must surely believe that they can have little in common.

What do all living things have in common?

Yet, all living things actually do have something in common. All living things are made of tiny units, called *cells*. The huge elephant is made of hundreds of billions of cells, and there are little animals whose whole body is but a single cell. The human body, too, is made of cells — billions of them.

Most cells are so small that you need

What do cells look like?

a powerful magnifying lens to see one. Some cells are so small that you could put 250 thousand of them on the period at the end of this sentence. Others, however, are large enough to be seen with the unaided eye. Among these large cells are the root-hairs of plants, certain seaweeds, and the eggs of animals.

Cells are of many shapes. Some are round. Others look like bricks with rounded corners. Still others are long and hairlike. Some cells are shaped like plates, cylinders, ribbons or spiral rods.

Looking through a microscope at a single cell from a human

What are the parts of a cell?

body, you can see that the cell is surrounded by membrane. This is the *cell membrane*. It surrounds the cell in the same way that a balloon surrounds the air within itself.

Within the cell membrane is a material that has a grainy appearance. This material is *cytoplasm*, which flows about within the cell membrane. Cytoplasm distributes nourishment within the cell and gets rid of the cell's waste products.

Within the cytoplasm is a large dot. This dot is really a sphere and is the cell's *nucleus*. The nucleus is the most important part of the cell. It directs

Tiny units are cells; a group of cells is a tissue; tissues form an organ; organs become unified system.

the cell's living activities. The way in which the cell uses nourishment and oxygen, the way the cytoplasm gets rid of wastes, the way the cell reproduces — all these functions are regulated by the nucleus. If the nucleus is removed, the cell dies.

The cell membrane, the cytoplasm,

Of what material are cells made?

and the nucleus of all cells are made of a material called *protoplasm*. Protoplasm is a living material and makes a living cell "alive." Scientists have analyzed protoplasm into the elements of which it is made. They have found protoplasm to

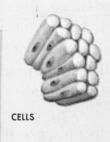
CELLS

TISSUE

ORGAN

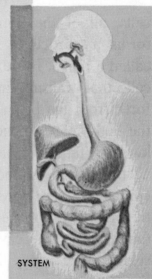
SYSTEM

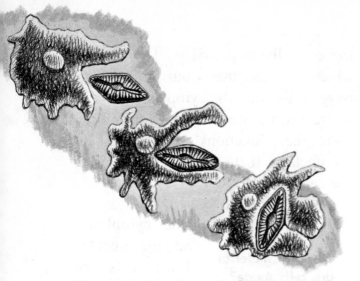

The amoeba is a microscopic mass of protoplasm. It is shown surrounding an organism on which it feeds.

be made of water and many other chemical substances. Although scientists know what these substances are and how much of each there is in protoplasm, no scientist thus far has been able to put them together properly so as to make living protoplasm. This fact tells us that protoplasm is a very complex material.

Cells not only differ in shape, but also in the work each

How are cells organized in a human body? kind of cell performs within a body. A group of cells, all of the same kind, that performs a particular kind of work, is called a *tissue*. For example, groups of cells that transmit impulses back and forth from the brain to other parts of the body make up nerve tissue. Other kinds of tissue are muscle tissue, connecting tissue, supporting tissue, and epithelial tissue. Epithelial tissue forms the outer layer of the skin, and the surface layer of the cavities in the body, such as the nose, throat, gullet and the stomach.

When different kinds of tissue are organized to perform a particular kind of work within a body, the tissues form an *organ*. An eye is an organ that performs the function of seeing. There are many parts to an eye and each part is made of a particular kind of tissue. When all the tissues of the eye work together while each tissue performs its separate task, then the eye can perform its function of seeing. Other examples of organs are the heart, liver, tongue and lungs.

Organs of the body are organized into unified *systems*. Each system performs a particular task for the body. For example, the digestive system, which includes the mouth, teeth, tongue, gullet, stomach, intestines and many glands, performs the function of digesting food.

Perhaps you have heard an automobile

How is the body like a machine? repairman say that a car's ignition system needed fixing. Or maybe it was the cooling system or the brake system. Each one of these systems is made up of several parts, and each system performs a particular task in running the car. All systems must work together if the car is to operate. Do you see the similarity between the automobile's systems and the organ systems of a human body?

The human body is a very wonderful machine. It is more complex, better made and can do more kinds of work under more conditions than any machine that man has so far constructed throughout his history.

Man has built giant electronic calculators that can solve mathematical problems in a fraction of the time that a human brain can. Calculating, however, is the only work the giant machine can do. It cannot decide what problems it should work on, nor when it should work on them, as the slower but more versatile human brain can. The great calculating machine, with its limited capacity, takes up all the space around the walls of a large room, but the human brain, with its unlimited capacity, can easily fit into a shoe box.

Why is the body more useful than a machine?

The calculating machine has thousands of parts, but the number of its parts does not even begin to equal the hundreds of millions of unit cells of which the human body is constructed. If the calculating machine breaks down, it must wait for a repairman to fix it. A break or a cut in some part of the human body can usually be repaired by the body itself.

Let us see in detail how this wonderful machine, the human body, works.

The Skin

When you look at a human body, the first thing you see is the *skin*. The average adult human body is covered with about eighteen square feet of skin. The skin varies in thickness. It is very thin over the eyelids, and quite thick on the palms of the hands and the soles of the feet.

How much skin is on a human body?

The skin is composed of two layers. The upper layer is the *epidermis*. This layer is made of dead, flattened cells, which are continually wearing off as we move around.

What are the parts of the skin?

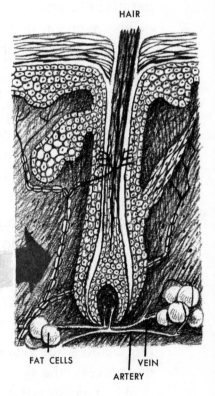

This is a cutaway view of a single hair (right) showing the follicle, which is the opening, or depression, from which the hair grows.

HAIR

FAT CELLS   VEIN   ARTERY

A cross section of human skin (left), shows the epidermis (top layer) and the dermis. The skin represents one of the largest organs of the entire human body.

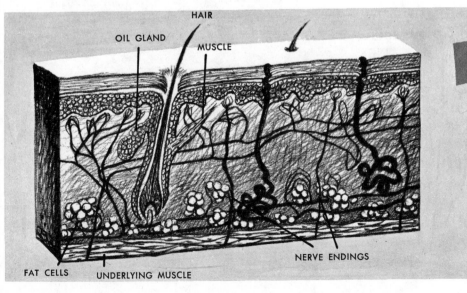

OIL GLAND   HAIR   MUSCLE

NERVE ENDINGS

FAT CELLS   UNDERLYING MUSCLE

The bottom of the epidermis is made of live cells that die and replace those that wear off on the surface.

Beneath the epidermis is the *dermis*. This layer of skin is made entirely of living cells. There are many small blood vessels and nerve endings in the dermis. Small coiled tubes in this layer open into the epidermis. These tubes are *sweat glands* and their openings are called *pores*. Hairs grow out of the skin and have their roots in the dermis. The openings from which hairs grow are called *hair follicles*.

The skin provides the body with a covering that is airtight, waterproof and, when unbroken, a bar to harmful bacteria.

What does the skin do?

The pigment, or coloring matter, of the skin screens out certain harmful rays of the sun.

The skin helps to regulate the temperature of the body. When the body surface is cold, the blood vessels in the skin contract and force blood deeper into the body. This prevents the body from losing much heat by radiation. When the body is too warm, the same blood vessels expand and bring more blood to the surface of the skin. This allows the body to lose heat by radiation. Also, the sweat glands pour out perspiration. The perspiration evaporates, and since evaporation is a cooling process, the skin is further cooled.

When perspiration flows out of the

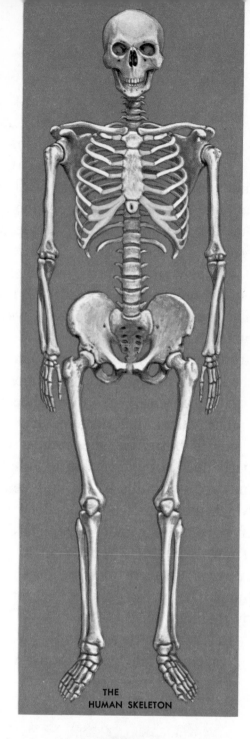

THE
HUMAN SKELETON

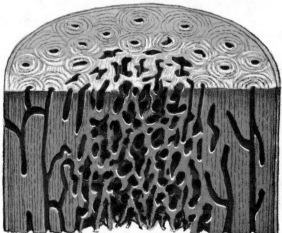

Cross section of human bone. Adults have 206 bones.

8

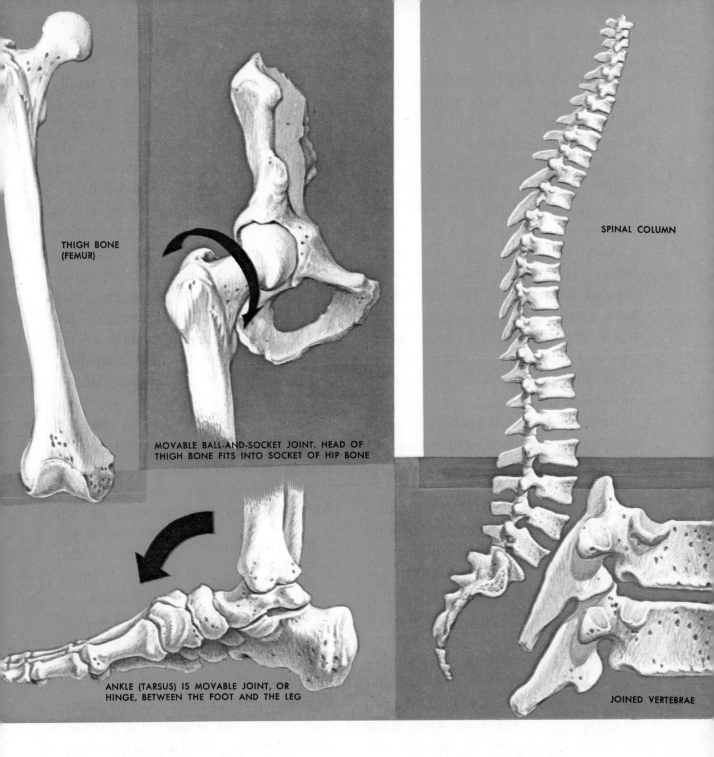

THIGH BONE
(FEMUR)

MOVABLE BALL-AND-SOCKET JOINT. HEAD OF
THIGH BONE FITS INTO SOCKET OF HIP BONE

ANKLE (TARSUS) IS MOVABLE JOINT, OR
HINGE, BETWEEN THE FOOT AND THE LEG

SPINAL COLUMN

JOINED VERTEBRAE

pores, it carries with it certain dissolved body wastes.

The skin is a sense organ because there are many nerve endings in the skin.

Although people do not ordinarily consider the skin to be an organ of the body, you can see by its structure and all the things it performs for the body that it really is an organ.

The Bones

What is the purpose of the skeleton?

If you suddenly removed the poles from a circus tent, the tent would collapse. The poles support the soft, pliable canvas of the tent. They also help to give the tent its shape. The *bones* of the human skeleton support the softer parts of the body

9

and give the body its general shape. If the skeleton of a body were suddenly removed, the body would sink to the floor in a shapeless mass.

The bones also help to protect the softer parts of the body. The skull forms a strong case for the very soft brain. Two bony sockets in front of the skull protect the eyes. The spinal column forms a bony tube that protects the delicate spinal cord. The ribs form a hard elastic framework that protects the heart and lungs. If a person had no ribs and bumped into someone, even a small bump might collapse the lungs or damage the heart.

Bones also provide anchors to which muscles are attached, and bones provide leverage for the movement of the muscles.

There are two other things that bones do for the body: the inner parts of some bones make blood cells; and bones are the body's chief storage place for calcium, a chemical element very important to the sound health of the body.

What is the structure of a bone? You can see, by looking at a cutaway view of a bone, that it consists of two main kinds of material: a dense outer material and a spongy, porous inner material. The hard outer material, that gives a bone its shape and strength, is made mostly of compounds of the chemical elements *calcium* and *phosphorus*. The soft inner part of the bone is called *marrow*. Most marrow is yellowish in color. It is made up of fat cells and is simply a storage depot for fat. Toward the ends of long bones, like those of the arms and legs, and generally throughout the interior of flat bones, such as those of the skull and the spinal column, there are patches and streaks of reddish tissue. This reddish tissue gets its color from red blood cells.

Long bones are generally cylindrical in shape. The long, cylindrical portion of these bones is called the *shaft*. The ends of the long bones are thicker than the shaft, and are shaped so that they may fit into the ends of adjoining bones. The short bones, such as those of the wrist and ankle, are composed mostly of a thick shaft of elastic, spongy material inside a thin covering of hard bone material. Flat bones, such as the ribs, are made up of spongy material between two plates of hard bone.

How many bones are there in the human body? An infant may have as many as 350 bones, but as the child grows older, many of these bones grow together to form single bones. A normal adult has 206 bones. Some adults may have a bone or two more, because the bones they had as infants did not grow together correctly. Some adults have a bone or two less, because the growing-together process went too far, and two bones of their ankles or wrists that should have remained separate may have grown together.

The skull is made up of twenty-nine bones. The round part of the skull, the part that encases the brain, is called the *cranium,* and consists of eight bones. The face, including the lower jaw, consists of fourteen bones. There are three tiny bones in each ear. And

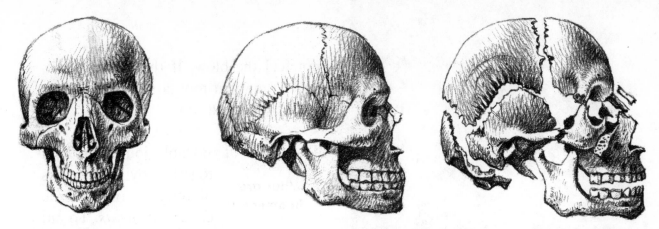

Front view of the human skull (left); side view (center); and side view with bones separated (right). The cranium, the part of the skull enclosing the brain, is composed of bones which are held together by immovable joints.

there is a single bone — the *hyoid bone* — in the throat.

The spinal column consists of twenty-six hollow cylinders of bone called *vertebrae*. If you strung together twenty-six spools of thread on a stiff wire in the shape of a very open letter S, you would have constructed something that looks much like the human spinal column.

The chest consists of twenty-five bones: one breast bone, called the *sternum,* and twenty-four ribs. Seven pairs of ribs attach to the spinal column at one end and the sternum at the other. Three pairs of ribs attach only to the spinal column, curve around to the front, but do not meet the sternum. And two pairs of ribs, called *floating ribs,* extend from the spine only part-way around to the front.

There are two collar bones, and two shoulder bones. Each arm consists of one upper-arm bone and two lower-arm bones. There are eight bones in the wrist. The palm of each hand is made up of five bones, and fourteen bones make up the fingers of a hand.

There are two hip bones. Each leg has one thigh bone, one kneecap, one shinbone, and one bone on the other side of the lower leg.

The ankle of each foot consists of seven bones and the foot, itself, of five, while fourteen bones make up the toes of each foot.

Every bone in the body — except one — meets with another bone. The one bone that does not meet another bone is the U-shaped hyoid bone in the throat.

How are the bones connected?

The meeting places of the bones are called *joints*. There are two kinds of joints: those about which the adjoining bones do not move, and those about which the bones do move freely. The bones of the cranium are held together by joints of the first kind. These are immovable joints.

Holding these bones together is a kind of very tough, springy tissue, called *cartilage*. Cartilage also joins together the bones of the spinal column. The springy nature of cartilage makes it a good shock absorber. If the lower parts of the spine receive a blow, the cartilage rings that join each vertebra to the one above it, absorb the shock, so that the brain does

What holds the bones together?

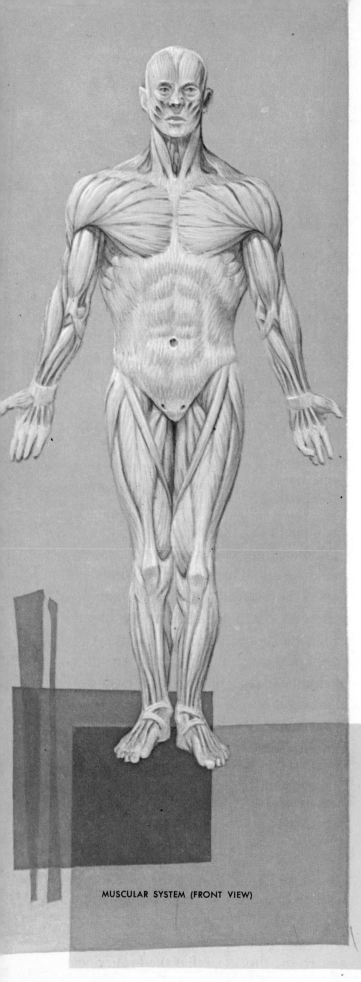

MUSCULAR SYSTEM (FRONT VIEW)

not feel the blow. If this were not so, every time you took a step, your brain would receive a jolt.

The bones at movable joints are held together by thick cords of tough, stringy tissue called *ligaments*. To aid movement, at least one of the two adjoining bones has a small hollow that contains a lubricating fluid. This fluid helps the bones move smoothly over one another, just as oil helps the parts of an engine move over one another.

What are ligaments?

All the bones of the body and their connecting cartilage and ligaments make up the body's *skeletal system*.

The Muscular System

The bones of the human body have no way of moving themselves. The muscles of the body move the bones and there are more than 600 muscles to move the parts of the skeleton. Muscles make up more than half the weight of the human body.

What are the muscles?

Muscles are made of bunches of

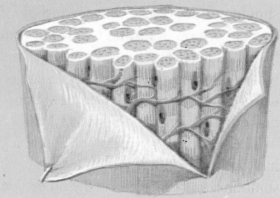

CROSS SECTION THROUGH MUSCLE

12

muscular tissue held tightly together. Muscular tissue is very fibrous, so that a muscle is somewhat like a bunch of rubber bands bound tightly together.

Beef is the muscle of steers. With a pin,

How can you see muscle fibers? pick apart a piece of roast beef. You will easily be able to separate it into long, thin strands that are fibers of muscle tissue. If you have a microscope, place a very thin muscle fiber under a cover-glass upon a glass slide. You will then be able to see that muscle tissue is made up of spindle-shaped cells.

A typical muscle is thick in the middle

How are muscles attached to bones? and tapers gradually toward the ends. It is the ends of a muscle that are attached to bones. One end of a muscle is anchored to a bone that the muscle cannot move. This attachment is called the *origin* of the muscle. The other end is attached to a bone that the muscle is intended to move. This attachment is called the *insertion* of the muscle. For example, the

MUSCULAR SYSTEM
(BACK VIEW)

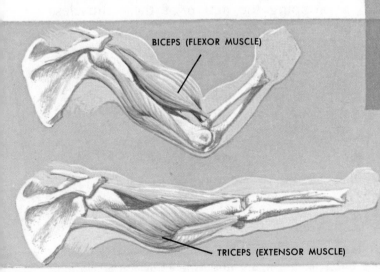

BICEPS (FLEXOR MUSCLE)

TRICEPS (EXTENSOR MUSCLE)

TENDONS AND LIGAMENTS OF KNEE JOINT

muscle at the front of the upper arm — called the *biceps* — has its origin at the shoulder bone, and its insertion is just below the elbow joint on the bone that is on the thumb side of the forearm. The actual attachment of the end of a muscle to a bone is usually accomplished by a short, tough cord of much the same kind of tissue that makes up ligaments. This connective cord is called a *tendon*.

All the muscles of the body and their tendons make up the *muscular system* of the body.

The muscles that move the skeleton are

What are the two kinds of muscle? ones that we can move at will. They are called *voluntary muscles*. Among them are the ones that move the eyes, tongue, soft palate and the upper part of the gullet.

There are muscles in the body that we cannot move at will. These are called *involuntary muscles*. This type of muscle is found in the walls of veins and arteries, stomach, intestines, gall bladder, the lower parts of the gullet and in several other internal organs. Thousands of tiny involuntary muscles in the skin move the hair. When you are chilled or frightened and have goose flesh, or goose pimples, the little lumps on your skin are due to the tiny muscles in the skin pulling your hairs erect.

The eye provides a good distinction be-

What are the differences in muscles? tween voluntary and involuntary muscles. Voluntary muscles enable you to control the movements of your eye, in order to look in the direction you wish. However, you cannot control at will the muscle that widens and narrows the pupil of your eye. This muscle is involuntary.

But the distinction between voluntary and involuntary muscles does not always hold true. For instance, when you shiver with cold or fright, the muscles that shake your body are voluntary muscles. Ordinarily, you can control these muscles, but , when shivering, you have no control over either starting or stopping the action of these muscles.

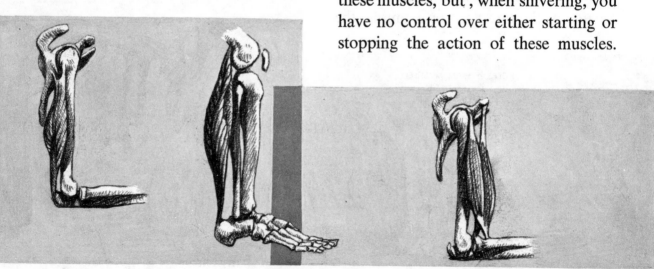

Lowering the arm (left) is an example of a first-class lever, as in a seesaw; rising on the toes (center), a second-class lever, as in a rowing oar; flexing, or "making a muscle" (right), a third-class lever, as in a fishing rod.

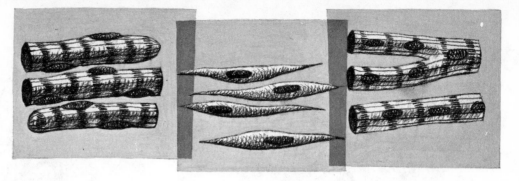

The stringlike matter making up voluntary muscles is known as fiber. Three kinds of muscle fiber are shown here (left to right): skeletal, smooth, cardiac.

They act as if they were involuntary. Certain circus performers can swallow various objects, and then, at will, bring them up without difficulty. These performers have learned to control their involuntary stomach and lower-gullet muscles, as though they were voluntary muscles.

Muscle tissue is made of cells whose cytoplasm can contract. When the muscle contracts, it becomes short, and thereby pulls on the bone in which it is inserted. When you want to show someone how strong you are and you "make a muscle" by contracting your biceps, your forearm is pulled up toward your shoulder. If you want to lower your arm, you relax your biceps and contract your *triceps,* the muscle on the underside of the arm. The contraction of the triceps pulls the forearm straight. You can see that the two muscles of the upper arm work as a team or pair. All the voluntary muscles of the body work in pairs.

How do muscles move?

One way to increase the power used to do work is to apply that power to a lever. A lever is a device that increases work power or range of motion. The joints in the human body act as

How do joints help muscles to move bones?

levers that increase the power of a muscle or increase the distance through which the muscle can move a bone.

If you raise yourself on your toes, you are making use of one kind of lever. The muscles that form the calves of your legs have to do the work of lifting your whole body. You would need to have much larger calf muscles if they had to undergo the strain of lifting your body by a direct pull. Yet you easily raise yourself on your toes, because your foot acts as a lever.

In the act of raising yourself on your toes, your weight bears straight down on the point where your shinbone rests on your ankle bone. The muscles of your calf pull upward on your heel bone, and your foot pivots upward on the fulcrum — the point around which the lever moves — which is formed by the bones that make up the ball of your foot. (Although we say that we raise ourselves on our toes, we actually raise ourselves on the balls of our feet and steady ourselves with our toes.)

If you reach down and grasp the back of your foot just above your heel, you can feel the strong tendon — called the *Achilles tendon*—that connects the muscles of your calf to your heel bone. If, now, you raise yourself on the ball of your foot, you can feel the calf muscles tighten and bulge as they contract and pull upward on your heel.

15

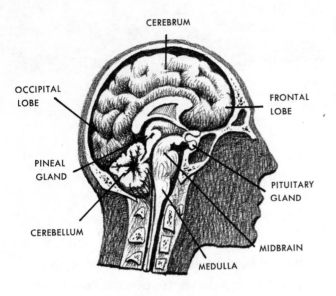

Cutaway view of the skull showing location of brain.

Parts of the brain control several of our activities.

The Brain and Nerves

Suppose you have dropped your pencil on the floor and want to pick it up.

What controls the movements of the body?

This is a very easy thing to do, something you can accomplish with hardly any thought or difficulty. Yet this simple action causes you to use dozens of your voluntary muscles.

First, you have to locate the pencil. This requires you to move your eyes, and probably also to turn your head, until you have brought the pencil into view. Then you must bend down to reach the pencil, grasp it, and then straighten up again. Not only do dozens of voluntary muscles bring about your motions, but they must do so in just the right order. It would be futile to attempt to grasp the pencil before you bent down to bring your hand within reach. Clearly something is controlling the motions of your muscles. What is it?

The movements of your muscles are controlled by your brain which works through a system of nerves distributed throughout your body. The brain and the nerves, together, make up the body's *nervous system*.

The brain occupies the upper half of the skull. The largest part of the brain, called the *cerebrum*, consists

What is the cerebrum?

of two deeply-wrinkled hemispheres of nerve tissue, one hemisphere on each side of the head.

All of man's conscious activities are controlled by his cerebrum. It enables him to remember, perceive things, solve problems and understand meanings — in short, to think. Thanks to man's most highly-developed cerebrum, he is the most intelligent of all animals.

At the back of the skull, and almost covered by the cere-

What is the cerebellum?

brum, is the *cerebellum*. This part of the brain, too, consists of two hemispheres.

16

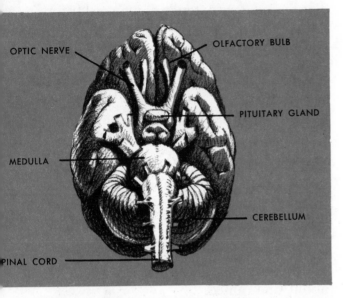

OPTIC NERVE

OLFACTORY BULB

PITUITARY GLAND

MEDULLA

CEREBELLUM

SPINAL CORD

An undersurface view of the brain showing its parts.

The brain and spinal cord make up the central nervous system. The nerves which branch out of this nervous system form the peripheral nervous system.

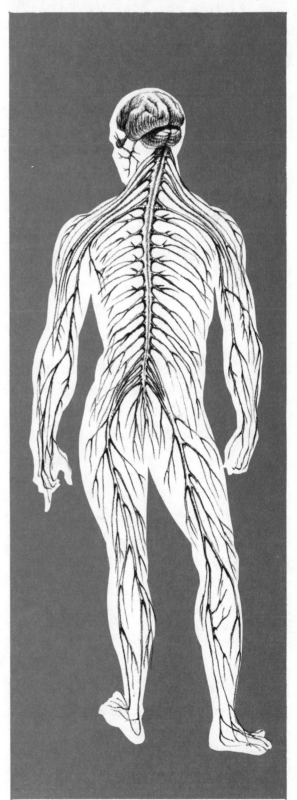

The cerebellum coordinates muscular activity. It is the cerebellum that is responsible for man's ability to learn habits and develop skills. As an infant you learned, after many tries and falls, to stand upright. Learning to walk was another accomplishment that took much time and effort. Now, standing and walking are habits to which you need give no thought, yet both these activities require the use of many muscles in exactly the right order. The cerebellum automatically controls these muscles.

Have you learned to skate or ride a bicycle? At first, you had to think about each move you made, but soon the movements became automatic, so that you did not have to think unless an unusual situation arose. When you were learning, your cerebrum was in control of your movements as you thought about just which muscles you were going to use next. Later, when you knew how to make each movement correctly, your cerebellum took over con-

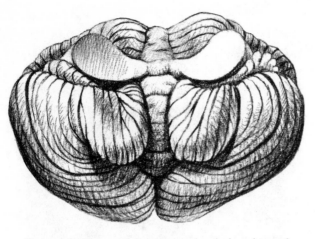

The cerebellum coordinates man's mind and muscles.

trol from your cerebrum. Although the cerebellum's muscular control is automatic, it is important to remember that the muscles it controls are voluntary muscles.

The involuntary muscles are controlled

What is the medulla?

by a small part of the brain that is at the top of the spinal cord. This is the *medulla*. It is a little more than an inch long and is really a thickening

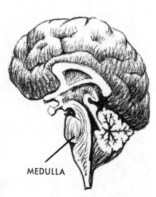

The medulla is a bulblike enlargement of the spinal cord. It carries and sends out nerve impulses which control circulation of blood, breathing, digestion and other processes, too.

MEDULLA

of the spinal cord. The medulla controls the beating of the heart, the rate of breathing, the movements of the stomach and intestines, the movements of the gullet when swallowing and other vital activities of the body.

The *spinal cord* extends downward from

What does the spinal cord look like?

the medulla through the protecting bony rings of the spinal column. The cord is cylindrical in shape, with an outer covering of supporting cells and blood vessels, and an inner, H-shaped core of nerve fibers. The spinal cord extends through four-fifths the length of the spine, and is a little longer in men than in women, averaging sixteen and one-half inches in length. It weighs just about one ounce.

Twelve pairs of nerves branch off the spinal cord and pass through the base of the skull into the brain. Thirty-one other pairs branch off the spinal cord throughout its length. These nerve branches run to all the organs of the body, where they branch again and again, until the smallest branches are nerves which are so thin that they cannot be seen with the unaided eye.

Nerves that extend upward from the spinal cord to the brain pass through the medulla where they cross. Thus, the left side of the brain controls the right side of the body, while the right side of the brain controls the left side of the body.

An army division is composed of many

How is the nervous system like an army telephone network?

thousands of men who perform a wide variety of duties. In order to control the activities of so many soldiers, it is necessary to have some system by which the commanding general can learn what is going on in all the units of his division and thus, to give orders to any of these units. In order to accomplish this, a telephone network is set up.

When a battle is in progress, soldiers posted near the battle line can telephone reports of action back to their headquarters in order to inform the general of the situation. The general gets the messages from these posts. Using this information, and calling on his training and experience, he issues orders to be followed by soldiers under his command. These orders travel back along the same telephone wires.

Let us follow a similar situation within the human body. Let us suppose that you have accidently knocked a pencil off your desk and want to pick it up. When the sound of the falling pencil reaches your ears, it causes elec-

trical impulses to move from your ears along two nerves — auditory nerves — and then to your brain. Your ears are similar to the posts near the battle line, your nerves similar to the telephone wires, and the electrical impulses similar to the messages that move along the wires.

When the brain receives electrical impulses from the ears, a particular part of the cerebrum perceives the impulses as sound, and passes this information on to another part of the cerebrum, one that is concerned with recognition. This part of the brain calls on the part that stores information —

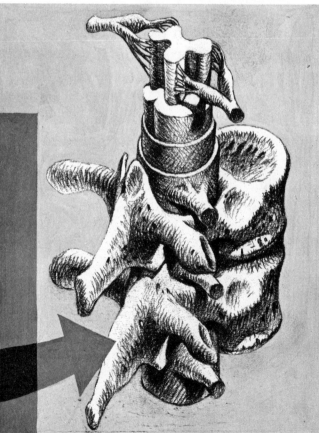

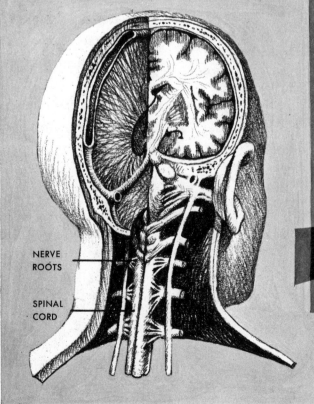

NERVE ROOTS

SPINAL CORD

(Left): Cutaway view of back of the head. (Above): Part of the backbone, also known as the spine, spinal column and vertebral column. It consists of bones called vertebrae which surround the spinal cord.

the memory. If you have ever before heard a pencil fall, your memory recognizes the sound. Now, you are aware of what has happened.

This situation is similar to that of the general who gets battle reports, and then calls on his training and past experience to help him get a clear picture of what is taking place at the battle-front.

Once your brain is aware of the fallen pencil, it decides to pick up the pencil. Electrical impulses go from your brain to the muscles of your eyes, which then move about seeking to bring the pencil into view. This is similar to that of the general who sends messages to front-line posts asking for more information on the battle.

When the pencil is brought into view, electrical impulses flash back to your cerebrum, which must again go through the processes of perception and recognition, in order to identify the pencil. Here we have new reports coming back to the commanding general who interprets them.

Having located the pencil, your cerebrum now sends hundreds of electrical impulses along nerves to the many muscles that must be moved when you bend over, reach out your arm, close your fingers around the pencil, and then straighten up again. These impulses and the responding muscular movements are similar to messages from the general going out over the telephone wires and the soldiers acting upon the general's orders.

Nerve cells, also called *neurons,* are **What are nerve cells?** specially constructed so as to carry nerve impulses from one part of the body to another. Nerve tissue can conduct extremely small amounts of electricity. Nerve impulses are actually small amounts of electricity.

Each neuron has a central portion, or **What are the parts of a neuron?** *cell body,* that has a nucleus, cytoplasm and a cell membrane. From one side of the cell body there extend very slender branching threads of protoplasm.

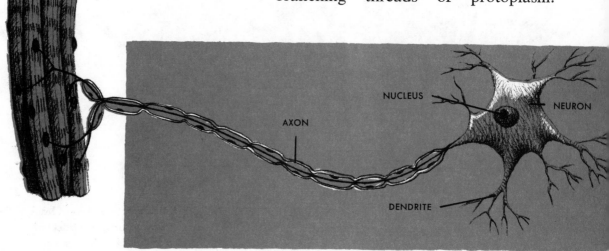

NUCLEUS

NEURON

AXON

DENDRITE

Nerve impulses from a neuron travel to the nerve endings of a muscle (left).

The nervous system of the human body operates in much the same manner as a telephone switchboard operation.

These tiny nerve fibers are called *dendrites*. They look much like twigs at the end of a tree branch. From the other side of the cell body there extends a fairly thick nerve fiber — surrounded by a fatty sheath — which ends in slender, branching threads of protoplasm. These nerve fibers are called *axons*. Some axons are very short, while others are as much as three feet long. Dendrites conduct nerve impulses to the cell body. Axons carry impulses away from the cell body.

Nerve tissue is made up of a series of neurons arranged so that the branching threads of protoplasm of an axon intermingle with the dendrites of the neighboring neuron. However, the two sets of branches do not actually touch. The gap between the branches is called a *synapse*. When an impulse moves along a nerve, it must jump across the syn-

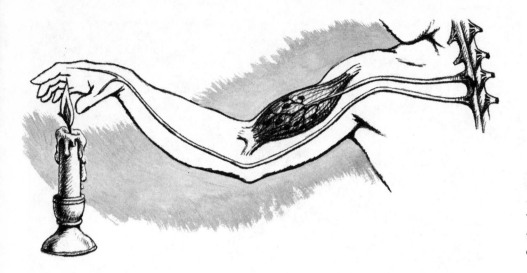

A simple reflex action takes place when you touch a candle flame. The arm muscles contract and you pull your arm away very quickly.

apse between one neuron and its neighbor.

Nerves are divided into two kinds: *sensory nerves* that carry impulses from sense organs to the brain, and *motor nerves* that carry command impulses to the muscles.

If you touch a very hot radiator, you quickly jerk your hand away. You do not think about pulling your hand away — you act automatically. This automatic action is called a *reflex action.*

What is a reflex action?

In a reflex action, the nerve impulse takes a special pathway, called a *reflex arc.* In the case of your touching the hot radiator, the impulse moved from the skin where it came in contact with the radiator along a sensory nerve to your spinal cord. Here the impulse set off another impulse in a motor nerve running from your spinal cord to your arm muscles. The muscles contracted and pulled your hand away from the radiator. This action took place in about one-tenth of a second.

At the same time, the original sensory impulse traveled up your spinal cord to your brain, where you felt it as pain.

Reflex actions are very useful in protecting the body from harm. If you had to think about what movements to make when suddenly threatened with harm, you might become confused and do the wrong thing. The automatic action of your reflexes usually causes you to act correctly and quickly enough to avoid or lessen the danger threatening you. For example, if you suddenly become aware of an object flying through the air toward your face, reflex actions cause you to dodge the object and to close your eyes tightly.

How are reflex actions helpful?

Sit comfortably in a chair, and cross your right leg over the upper part of your left leg. Feel around just below the kneecap of your right leg for a tendon

How can you demonstrate a reflex action?

that runs downward from the kneecap. With the edge of the fingers of your right hand strike this tendon sharply — though not too hard, of course. If you do this correctly, the lower part of your right leg will jump upward, bending from the knee joint. After you have learned to cause this reflex action, wait a few minutes and try it again. This time, you may note that your leg is already in motion before you feel your fingers strike the knee.

The Senses

What are the senses? We are made aware of the world around us by means of our *senses*. For many centuries, man believed that human beings had only five senses: *sight, hearing, touch, smell,* and *taste*. Modern scientists have added to the list the senses of *pressure, heat, cold* and *pain*.

There are several steps in the process of sensing. A stimulus acts on the nerves in one of the sense organs. Nerve impulses from the sense organ travel to the brain. In the brain, the impulses are interpreted as a feeling or sensation. For instance, if you stick your finger with a needle, nerve endings in the skin of your finger are stimulated to send impulses to your brain, which interprets the impulses as pain.

It is important to note that, although the brain interprets the impulses as pain, the pain is not felt in the brain, but rather in the finger; that is, the sense organ.

CROSS SECTION OF THE HUMAN EYE

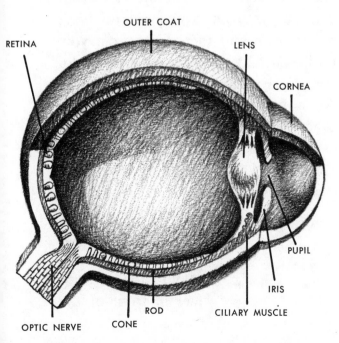

RETINA

OUTER COAT

LENS

CORNEA

PUPIL

IRIS

OPTIC NERVE   CONE   ROD   CILIARY MUSCLE

What does the eye look like? The organs of sight are the *eyes*. A human eye is shaped like a ball and is about an inch in diameter. The eye is surrounded by a tough white protective covering. At the front of the eye, there is a transparent circular portion in this covering. Just behind this transparent portion is a space filled with a clear liquid. At the back of this space is a circular tissue with a hole in it. The tissue is called the *iris,* and the hole is the *pupil*. The iris is the colored part of the eye. On the

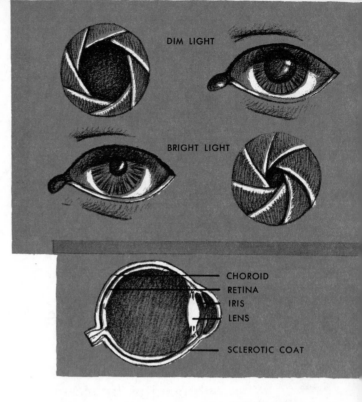

DIM LIGHT

BRIGHT LIGHT

CHOROID
RETINA
IRIS
LENS

SCLEROTIC COAT

inner edge of the iris, around the pupil, is a ring of tiny muscles sensitive to light. In bright light, these muscles contract and narrow the pupil. In dim light, the muscles relax and widen the pupil.

If you stand in front of a mirror in a brightly-lit room, you can easily see the pupil of your eye widen and narrow. Cover one eye with your hand for about a minute and a half. Suddenly remove your hand, and look at the eye that was covered. You will see the pupil narrow.

Behind the iris is a transparent circular lens made of tough tissue. **How do we see?** Muscles attached to the rim of this lens can focus it upon near or far objects. A beam of light passing through the lens is turned upside down and is reversed from right to left. After passing through the lens, light traverses a large spherical cavity that makes up the bulk of the eye. This cavity is filled with a clear liquid through which light passes easily. Around the inner surface of this cavity is a coating of special nerve endings that are sensitive to light. This sensitive coating is the *retina*. The nerve endings connect with the *optic nerve* that leads to the brain.

Light, reflected from an object and entering the eye, is focused by the lens as a reversed image on the retina. The nerve impulses arriving at the brain from the retina are interpreted as an image of the object.

This interpretation also reverses the directions of the image as it was projected on the retina, so that we do not see things upside down and backward.

At the point where the optic nerve enters the eye, there is **What is the blind spot?** no retina, and consequently, this area is not light-sensitive. This point, which is just below the center of the back of the eye, is called the *blind spot*.

You can prove the existence of this blind spot in the following manner. Note the cross and the dot on this page. Close your left eye, and hold this page before your open right eye. Fix your gaze on the cross. Now move the book toward you and then away from you, until you find the point where the dot completely disappears. At this point the dot is focused by the lens of the eye exactly on your blind spot. Hence, you can't see the dot.

✚   ●

Place a table directly beneath a light, so that objects near **Why do we see better with two eyes than with one?** the center of the table cast no shadows. Stand about eight feet in front of the

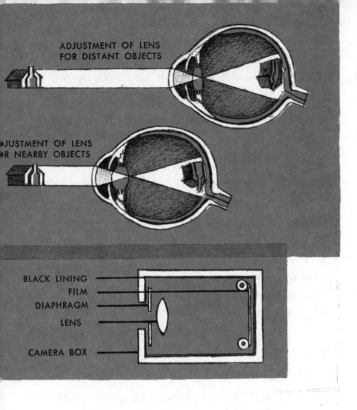

ADJUSTMENT OF LENS
FOR DISTANT OBJECTS

ADJUSTMENT OF LENS
FOR NEARBY OBJECTS

BLACK LINING
FILM
DIAPHRAGM
LENS

CAMERA BOX

The characteristics and operation of both the human eye and the camera eye show remarkable similarity.

vide the viewer with a perception of depth that enables him to make judgments of farness and nearness. This is why you had a better score when judging the locations of the spools with both eyes open.

The *ears* are the organs of hearing. The

What does the ear look like?

part of the ear on the outside of the head helps to a slight extent to direct sound waves into the ear. Sound waves entering the ear strike the eardrum, or *tympanic membrane,* and cause it to vibrate. This membrane stretches taughtly across the whole diameter of the ear passage. Touching the inner surface of the eardrum is a tiny bone called the *malleus* or hammer. The malleus connects by a joint to another little bone, the *incus* or anvil. And the incus is jointed to a third bone, the *stapes* or stirrup — so named because it looks like a stirrup. Below

table. Crouch down so that your eyes are on a level with the top of the table, and close one eye.

Ask someone to stand a thread-spool at the center of the table. Also ask him to place another spool of the same size about four inches in front or in back of the first spool, but not to tell you whether the second spool is before or behind the first. Try to guess the location of the second spool. Try this several times, keeping a record of your correct guesses. You will probably have a poor score.

With both eyes open, repeat your guessing. This time, you should have a nearly-perfect score. Why?

When we look at an object with both eyes, a slightly different image is projected on the retina of each eye. This is true because each eye sees the object from a slightly different angle. The result is that the brain's interpretation of the two images provides the viewer with a single, three-dimensional image of the object. The two images also pro-

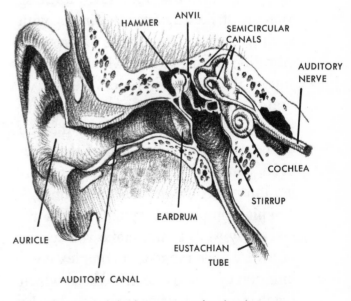

HAMMER ANVIL
SEMICIRCULAR CANALS
AUDITORY NERVE
COCHLEA
STIRRUP
EARDRUM
EUSTACHIAN TUBE
AURICLE
AUDITORY CANAL

A cross section of the human ear, showing its parts.

25

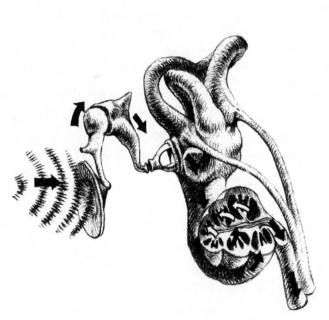

Arrows show path of sound through the inner ear.

presence of an orchestra. Also, your hearing organs can be activated by such small volumes of sound as those which come from a pencil moving over a sheet of paper on the other side of a room from the hearer.

Blindfold yourself with a handkerchief, and sit on a chair placed in the middle of a room. Ask someone to move quietly to any part of the room and clap his hands once. Point to where you think he is. Repeat this activity several times as your aide moves quietly from place to place about the room. Have your helper keep score of the number of times you have pointed correctly to the location at which he clapped his hands.

Why do we hear better with two ears than with one?

Place a hand tightly over one ear, and repeat the whole experiment. Repeat it a third time, covering the other ear.

If your sense of hearing is normal, you will find that your score of correct locations was poorer when you listened with only one ear. From this you can readily understand that using two ears gives you a better perception of sound direction, just as using two eyes gives you a better perception of visual depth.

and inward from the stirrup are three small cavities filled with liquid that are separated from each other by membranes. The innermost of these membranes connects with nerves that go to the brain.

When sound waves cause the eardrum to vibrate, the eardrum causes the malleus to vibrate, too. The vibrating malleus strikes against the incus with each vibration. The incus passes the vibration to the stirrup, which, in turn, causes the liquid in the cavities to vibrate. Vibration in the innermost cavity sets up impulses in the nerves that go to the cerebrum. That part of the cerebrum concerned with the sense of hearing interprets the impulses as sound.

How do we hear?

This complicated system works remarkably well. It can make you aware of a very wide range and complex combination of sounds, such as those which reach your ear when you are in the

The organ of smell is the *nose*. When taking a breath, you may draw into your nose certain gases intermingled with the gases of which air is made. When the added gases come into contact with a small patch of epithelial cells on the upper part of the

Why do we smell odors?

inner surface of your nose, the cells cause impulses to travel along a pair of nerves to your cerebrum, where the impulses are interpreted as odors.

Just how this process takes place is not clearly known. However, since the inside of the nose is always damp, scientists believe that the odorous gases dissolve in the dampness and cause a chemical reaction that stimulates nerve endings in the epithelial cells. This causes the cells to send impulses along the nerves.

Not all gases react with the organ of smell to set up sensations of odor. This is why we call only certain gases — those that do react — odors or smells. The more of an odorous gas that comes into contact with the organ of smell, the stronger is the sensation of odor. This is why we usually draw deep breaths when we sniff about to locate the source of an odor.

Can the sense of smell get "tired" or "lost"? The sense of smell seems to become fatigued easily; that is, the sensation of odor fades after a short time. Perhaps you have entered a room in which you found a strong odor. After a few minutes, however, you did not seem to notice the odor at all.

The discharge of mucus that accompanies a severe cold will cause you to lose your sense of smell, because the mucus forms a thick covering over the epithelial cells of the nose and prevents odorous gases from coming in contact with the cells.

The sense of smell is highly developed among a large part of the animal kingdom. These animals use smell as their chief means of learning about their surroundings. In human beings, however, the sense of smell is only mildly developed.

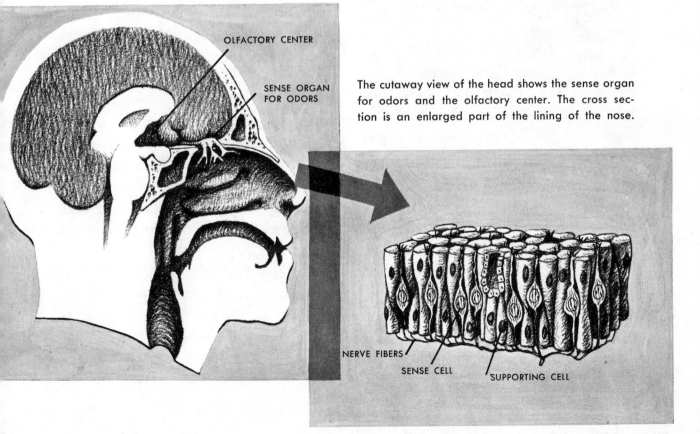

The cutaway view of the head shows the sense organ for odors and the olfactory center. The cross section is an enlarged part of the lining of the nose.

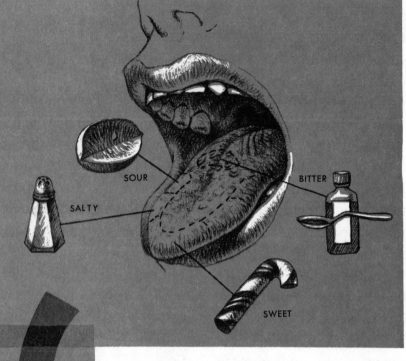

Different taste buds in the tongue are responsible for different taste sensations.

SOUR

SALTY

BITTER

SWEET

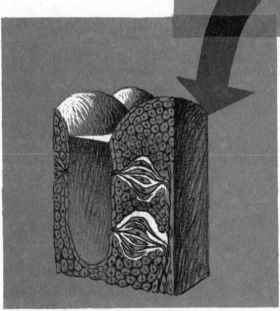

Taste buds are shown in this cross section of tongue.

Small organs, called *taste buds*, are lo-

How do we taste things?

cated just below the surface of the tongue and in three places in the throat. Certain materials taken into the mouth cause taste buds to produce the sensation of taste. Just how this sensation is brought about is not known. Taste, like smell, is probably the result of a mild chemical reaction. Taste sen-

sations may be divided into *sweet, salty, sour* and *bitter*.

Not all tastes are detected by the same taste buds. Those taste buds at the sides and tip of the tongue transmit impulses of saltiness to the brain. The buds at the tip of the tongue detect sweetness, those near the base detect bitterness and those on the sides detect sourness. Thus, there are certain areas of the tongue in which two kinds of taste buds are located: these are the sides and the tip.

The sense of taste is complicated by the fact that one taste may mask or counteract another. For example, the sweetness of sugar will counteract the sourness of lemon juice.

Taste is further complicated by the fact that certain tastes are actually odors. This is true of the taste of an onion. If a bad cold causes you to lose your sense of smell, you will not be able to taste an onion.

How do we feel things? The chief organs of feeling are free nerve endings in the epithelial cells of the body. On the outside of the body, the skin is the organ of feeling; within the body, it is the epithelial cells that line all cavities, such as the mouth, throat, stomach, intestines, ears, chest and sinuses.

Not all feelings are detected by the same nerve endings. In the skin there are 16,000 that detect heat and cold and more than four million that detect pain. Still others cause the sensation of touch. This latter sensation is in some way heightened by the hairs of the body. If a hairy portion of the body is shaved, its sensitivity to touch is temporarily reduced.

Sensations of feeling within the body are difficult to explain. Gas that distends the intestine during an attack of indigestion may cause intense pain. Yet surgeons have found that they can cut, burn, pinch and mash the internal organs of a person without causing the patient any pain.

Are all areas of the skin equally sensitive to the touch? Blindfold yourself. Ask someone to press lightly the blunt point of a pencil on the upturned palm of your hand. Have him repeat this action, using the points of two pencils held about a quarter of an inch apart. Let your helper continue to do this, alternating irregularly between one and two pencil points. As he does this, try to guess how many points are pressing on your hand each time. You will probably make a fairly good score of correct guesses.

But if you repeated this experiment, using the skin of your upper back, close to your spine, you would not be able to tell whether one or two pencil points were being used. This demonstrates that not all areas of the skin are equally sensitive to touch.

COLD

DEEP PRESSURE

LIGHT TOUCH

TOUCH

HEAT

PAIN

The skin is the organ of feeling. The cross sections show the nerve endings responsible for various sensations.

The Digestive System

We have learned that the blood carries nourishment to the cells of the tissues. This nourishment comes from the food we eat. Certainly, food in the form in which we put it into our mouths could not be carried by the blood. Before food is in a form that enables it to nourish the tissues, it must be greatly changed. This process of change is called *digestion*.

How does the body use food?

The mouth, esophagus (or gullet), stomach, small intestine and large intestine form a continuous tube about thirty feet long called the *alimentary canal*. Food passes through the alimentary canal during the process of digestion. The *liver* and the *pancreas,* two large glands, are also important in the digestion of food. The alimentary canal and these two glands make up the body's *digestive system*.

One of the constituents of food is starch. When food that contains starch is chewed, the saliva in the mouth brings about a chemical change in the starch. As a result of this change, the starch becomes a kind of sugar that is easy for the body to use as nourishment for the cells.

How does digestion begin in the mouth?

A substance, such as saliva, that changes food into a form that can be used by the body is called an *enzyme*. Enzymes are secreted by glands. Saliva is secreted by saliva glands in the roof and floor of the mouth.

Only starch can be digested in the mouth. Fats and proteins, the two other main constituents of food, must be digested farther along in the alimentary canal.

Since food, whether digested in the mouth or other part of the alimentary canal, must be swallowed, the food must first be broken up into small pieces. As we chew, our teeth cut and grind food into small pieces that are wetted by saliva, and finally formed by the tongue into lumps that we can easily swallow.

How do teeth aid digestion?

A tooth is a remarkable structure. The part of the tooth above the gum is the *crown;* below the crown, and covered by the gum, is the *neck;* below the neck is the *root* that lies in the socket of the jaw bone. A tooth has an outside covering of enamel, the hardest material in the body. Inside the enamel, and forming the main part of the tooth, is *dentine.* It looks like bone but is harder. In a cavity in the center of the tooth is the *pulp,* which contains blood vessels and nerves.

When you look on the shelves of a supermarket, you see such a variety of food that it is hard to believe all the different kinds can be divided into a few food elements. But this is true.

What are carbohydrates?

One food element is called *carbohydrate*. Carbohydrates are made up of the chemical elements carbon, hydrogen and oxygen. Starches and sugars, bread and macaroni and rock candy, too, are some carbohydrates. The human body uses carbohydrates as a source of energy. If the body has more carbohydrates than it can use, it may change them into fat, which it stores.

Another food element is *fat,* which is

What is fat?

a better source of energy than carbohydrate. Butter, margarine, lard and olive oil are a few examples of fat as well as the white irregular streaks in a beefsteak and around the edges of the steak.

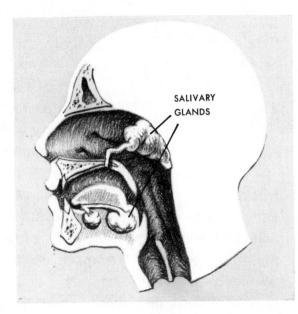

Location of the salivary glands in the human body.

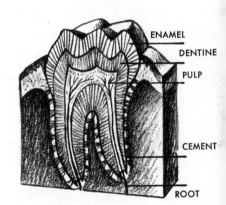

Cross section of a tooth.

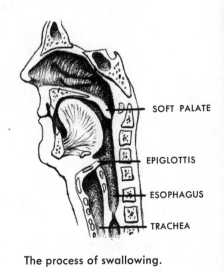

The process of swallowing.

	FOOD SOURCES	BENEFITS FOR BODY	RESULTS WHEN LACKING
A	Yellow and Green Vegetables	Growth — Eyesight	Night Blindness
B₁	Peanuts — Pork	Appetite — Nerves	Poor Appetite
B₂	Liver and Lean Meats	Burns Starches and Sugars	Lip Corners Crack
NIACIN	Wheat Bread — Greens	Healthy Skin	Upset Higher Centers of Brain
C	Strawberries, Red Peppers, Lemon Juice	Healthy Gums	Bleeding Gums
D	Sunshine — Cod Liver Oil	Prevents Rickets	Rickets
PROTEIN	Meat, Kidney Beans, Eggs	Growth	Mental, Physical Inefficiency
CALCIUM	Milk — Swiss Cheese	Formation of Teeth and Bones	Softening of Bones
IRON	Liver — Egg Yolks	Builds Red Blood Cells	Anemia
CALORIES	Butter, Sugar, Wheat Bread	Energy	Fatigue

31

If the body has more fat than it can use for energy, it stores it. That is why some people are stout.

The third main food element is *protein*

What is protein? which is manufactured in the bodies of green plants. When human beings or cattle eat green plants, the plant protein is changed into muscle. When human beings eat meat, which is cattle muscle, they make use of their best source of protein. Meat, also, builds muscle in the human body.

Many foods contain small amounts of

What are vitamins? substances called *vitamins,* which are necessary to the health of the body. Vitamins are named by means of the letters A, B, C, D, and K.

Vitamin A is important for healthy eyes, skin, mucous membranes and for normal growth. Vitamin B is needed for good appetite, good digestion of carbohydrates, normal growth and health of nerves and muscles. Vitamin C is important for growth, the development of teeth, good skin and healing. Vitamin D is needed for strong bones and teeth. Vitamin K is important for the clotting of blood and normal liver function.

Even if we eat enough food, we will not be healthy unless the food contains sufficient vitamins.

Other food elements are called *minerals.*

What are minerals? These are small amounts of certain chemical elements. For example, the elements phosphorus and calcium are needed for healthy teeth and bones.

In order to be healthy, we must give our bodies proper amounts of these food elements. How are we to know just what foods will provide the right amounts? Scientists have worked out the answers, and when our diet includes the proper amounts of each food element, we are then said to be eating a *balanced diet.*

A balanced diet will give the body the nourishment it needs. This is a requirement to maintain good health. A diet that is lacking in certain requirements could lead to a state of unhealth which doctors call *malnutrition.*

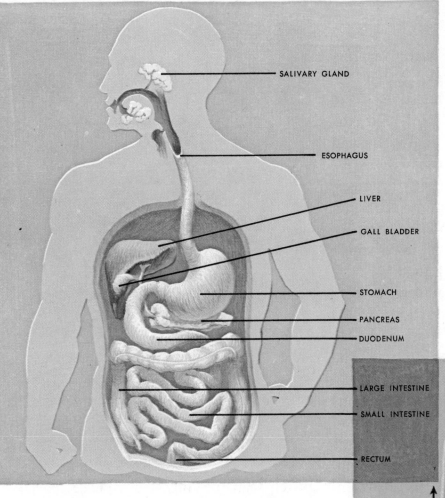

SALIVARY GLAND

ESOPHAGUS

LIVER

GALL BLADDER

STOMACH

PANCREAS

DUODENUM

LARGE INTESTINE

SMALL INTESTINE

RECTUM

The alimentary canal (including the mouth, esophagus, stomach, small and large intestines), the liver and the pancreas make up the body's digestive system.

A chicken sandwich, for example, con-

What is the process of digestion?

tains starch, fat and protein. The bread is mainly starch, the butter is fat and the chicken is protein.

When a piece of the sandwich is chewed, the starch is being digested by saliva.

When a mouthful of the sandwich is swallowed, it passes into the *esophagus*. This is the muscular tube that contracts along its length to push the food down into the stomach.

In the stomach, which is a muscle, the food is churned about while digestive juices pour in from glands in the stomach wall. Eventually, the churning action moves food out of the stomach and into the small intestine.

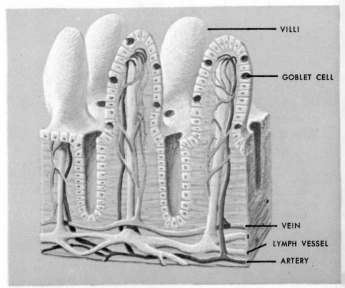

ACID

SECRETIN

SECRETIN

PROSECRETIN

ACID FOOD

FOOD

The stomach and intestine in the digestive process.

Digested food is absorbed through threadlike villi.

VILLI

GOBLET CELL

VEIN

LYMPH VESSEL

ARTERY

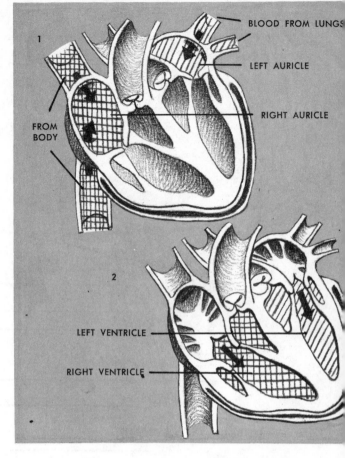

What does the small intestine do? The greater part of the digestive process takes place in the small intestine. Here the protein and the fat are finally changed into forms that can be used by the tissues. The liver contributes to this digestive process by secreting into the small intestine a liquid called *bile*. The pancreas secretes pancreatic juice which further aids in dissolving food.

The small intestine undergoes continual muscular contraction called *peristalsis*. This action pushes the digested food into the large intestine. The surface of the small intestine has a large number of threadlike projections called *villi*. The digested, liquefied food is absorbed through the villi, and passes into capillaries that are inside the villi. Now, the food is in the bloodstream. As we have learned, the blood carries the food to the cells in the tissues, which use the food to provide the body with energy and material for repair.

Not all the parts of the chicken sandwich can be digested. Those parts which are indigestible pass through the large intestine to its lower part, called the *rectum*. Eventually, the indigestible food is eliminated from the rectum through the *anus*.

The Circulatory System

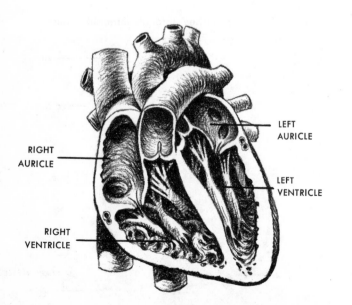

What work does the heart do? Although the study of anatomy is more than 2,000 years old, it was not until the English physician William Harvey described the circulation of the blood, at the beginning of the 17th century, that men knew what work the *heart* did in the body. The heart had been carefully dissected and described, yet no one knew its use.

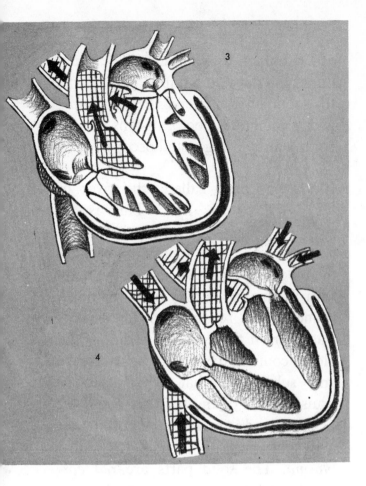

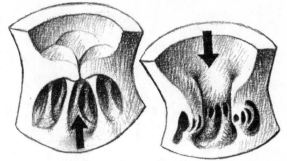

The arrows indicate the direction of blood pressure. Pressure forces closing and opening of the valves.

(1) Auricles contract, squeezing blood into ventricles. (2) Ventricles contract, cuspid valves close, semilunar valves open, blood goes to arteries. (3) Ventricles relax, semilunar valves close, cuspid valves open, blood goes to ventricles. (4) Blood goes to auricles and ventricles, heart relaxes, pauses momentarily.

The heart is a very efficient pump that moves blood through the body. The heart is a muscle that contracts and relaxes about seventy times a minute, for all the minutes of all the years of your life. Each contraction and relaxation of the heart muscle is a *heartbeat*. You have more than 100,000 heartbeats every day. Each heartbeat pumps about two ounces of blood. This results in about 13,000 quarts of blood being pumped each day.

What does the heart look like? The heart is divided into four chambers. The upper two chambers are called *auricles;* the lower two are called *ventricles*. Each auricle is connected with the ventricle below it by a valve that allows blood to flow from the auricle to the ventricle, but not in the opposite direction. The heart also contains a network of nerves that naturally regulates the pumping operation.

One of the wonders of modern surgery is the heart transplant, first demonstrated to be operationally feasible in humans by Dr. Christian Barnard. By this means, the deteriorated heart of a patient who would otherwise not have long to live may be physically replaced by the healthy heart of a person who has just died. Several people have been able to resume normal lives, thanks to this medical miracle.

How can you hear a heartbeat? Obtain two small funnels and a length of rubber tubing about one or two feet long. Into each end of the tube, place the snout of one of the funnels.

Now, place the rim of one funnel on the chest of a friend, and place the

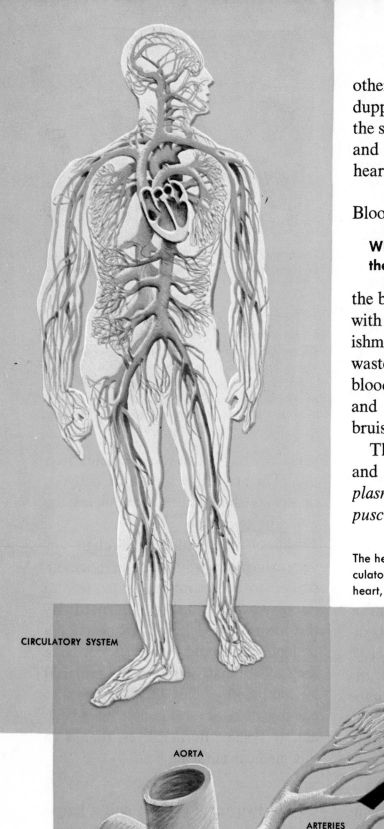

CIRCULATORY SYSTEM

other funnel to your ear. The "lub-dupp, lub-dupp, lub-dupp" you hear is the sound of your friend's heart opening and closing. A doctor listens to the heartbeat by using a stethoscope.

Blood has been called "the river of life." This is an appropriate description, because the blood supplies the cells of the body with the materials they need for nourishment and repair, and it removes wastes from the cells. In addition, the blood contains cells that fight disease and substances that repair cut or bruised parts of the body.

What work does the blood do?

The blood is made up of both liquid and solid parts. The liquid is called *plasma*. The solid parts are *red corpuscles, white corpuscles* and *platelets*.

The heart, blood, veins and arteries make up the circulatory system. The aorta carries the blood from the heart, which branch arteries distribute through body.

AORTA

VEINS

ARTERIES

VEIN

The word *corpuscle* is the Latin word for "little body."

More than nine-tenths of the blood con-
What are red corpuscles? sists of red corpuscles. They are so small that a large
drop of blood contains more than 250
million of them. They are disc-shaped
and concave on each side. These
corpuscles contain a substance called
hemoglobin, which is a compound of
iron. Hemoglobin can combine very
well with oxygen from the air in the
lungs. It is the task of the red corpuscles to carry oxygen to cells in all parts
of the body, and upon reaching these
cells, to give up the oxygen to them.

When hemoglobin combines with
oxygen, it turns bright red. That is why
blood running out of a cut is always
red — the hemoglobin is combining
with the oxygen of the air.

Red corpuscles live only about fifty
to seventy days, and thus, they must be
replaced continuously. We learned that
the interior of a bone contains reddish
tissue, which is due to the presence of
red blood cells. Within the marrow of
some bones, red cells are formed.

If a person lacks sufficient red cor-

Red corpuscles, white corpuscles and platelets make up the solid part of the blood, as opposed to plasma.

The cross sections, below, demonstrate how the human body uses its own substances to heal surface wounds.

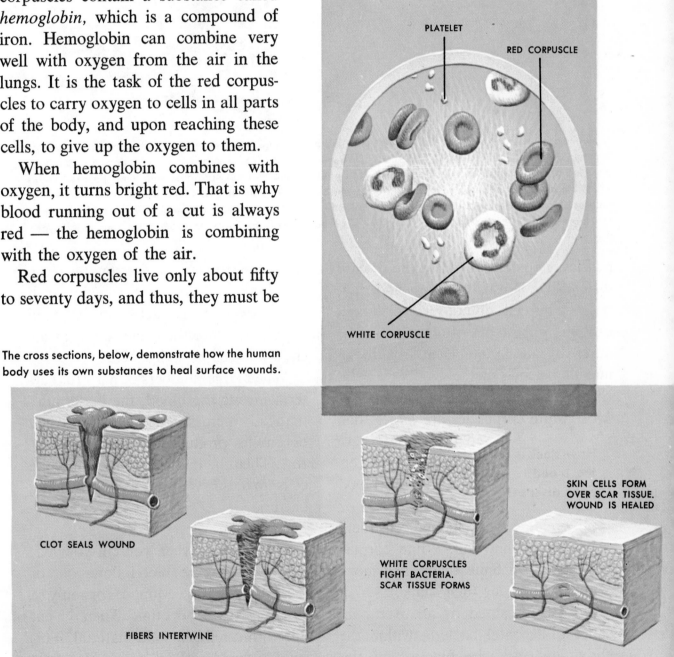

PLATELET

RED CORPUSCLE

WHITE CORPUSCLE

CLOT SEALS WOUND

FIBERS INTERTWINE

WHITE CORPUSCLES FIGHT BACTERIA. SCAR TISSUE FORMS

SKIN CELLS FORM OVER SCAR TISSUE. WOUND IS HEALED

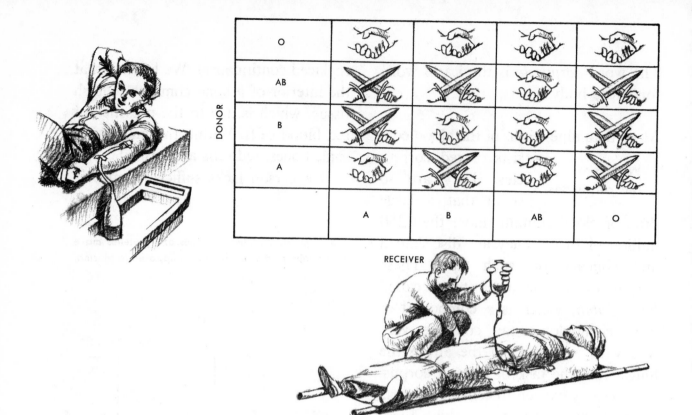

A Nobel prize-winning scientist, Karl Landsteiner, discovered that there were four main groups of blood in humans, which he classified as A, B, AB and O. This is important because in a blood transfusion, a person with one kind of blood would become ill if he received another kind that did not agree with him. The chart shows which blood types can be given in transfusion to persons with any of the four blood groups. It also shows the type of blood that persons with any of the four blood groups can receive. The symbol of the handshake stands for "agree with." The crossed swords signify "opposed to." All the races have the same four blood types.

puscles, he is said to have the disease *anemia.* He is usually listless and thin, because his cells do not receive enough oxygen. Some types of anemia may be cured by adding sufficient iron to an anemic person's diet.

Most white corpuscles are larger than

How does the blood fight disease? red ones, and there are fewer white corpuscles in the blood than red ones. For

approximately every 800 red cells there is only one white cell. White corpuscles have no definite shape, and move about by changing their shape.

Disease is caused by an overabundance of harmful bacteria within the body, and it is the function of the white corpuscles to destroy bacteria. To destroy a bacterium, a white cell moves over to the bacterium and then engulfs it. Once the bacterium is inside the white cell, it is digested.

When large numbers of harmful bacteria invade the blood, the body automatically increases the number of white corpuscles produced by the bone marrow. Then the body has sufficient white cells to destroy most of the invading bacteria.

You know that when you cut yourself,

How does blood clot? the blood flows out of the wound for only a short time. Then the cut

fills with a reddish solid material. This solid is called a *blood clot.* If blood did

38

not clot, anyone with even a slight wound would bleed profusely. Indeed, the blood of certain persons does not clot, a condition known as *hemophilia*.

The platelets are the particles in the blood responsible for causing it to clot. When blood flows from a cut, it carries platelets. When air comes into contact with the platelets, the oxygen in the air causes the platelets to disintegrate and release a substance that combines with certain substances in the plasma. This combination forms a substance called *fibrin*. Fibrin is in the form of a network of tiny threadlike fibers that trap the cells of the blood to form a dam which holds back the further flow of blood.

Since the heart pumps so much blood, it must be clear

How does blood move through the body?

that the same blood must pass through the heart many times in the course of a day. This is true, for the round trip of blood from the heart to distant parts of the body and back takes less than a minute. The round trip to nearer parts of the body takes an even shorter time.

The blood takes two main paths in its trip through the body. When the right ventricle of the heart contracts, blood is forced into a large artery that leads to the lungs. (An *artery* is an elastic tube that carries blood away from the heart.) Here the red cells of the blood take up oxygen from the air in the lungs. They also give up carbon dioxide.

From the lungs, the blood flows through two veins that lead back to the heart. (A *vein* is an elastic tube that carries blood toward the heart.) The blood enters the left auricle and passes through the valve leading to the left ventricle. When the left ventricle contracts, the blood flows into another large artery. This artery branches into smaller arteries that branch several times more into smaller and smaller arteries. The smallest arteries are in the tissues, and are called *capillary* arteries. From the capillaries, the blood transfers nourishment and oxygen to the cells and removes carbon dioxide and other wastes.

Capillary arteries connect with capillary veins. These tiny veins connect with larger and larger veins as they approach nearer to the heart. Blood flowing through the veins eventually reaches a large vein that enters the right auricle of the heart. From the right auricle, the blood flows through the valve leading to the right ventricle, and thus it ends a complete round trip through the body.

The heart, the blood and the veins and arteries make up the body's *circulatory system*.

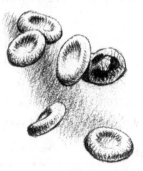

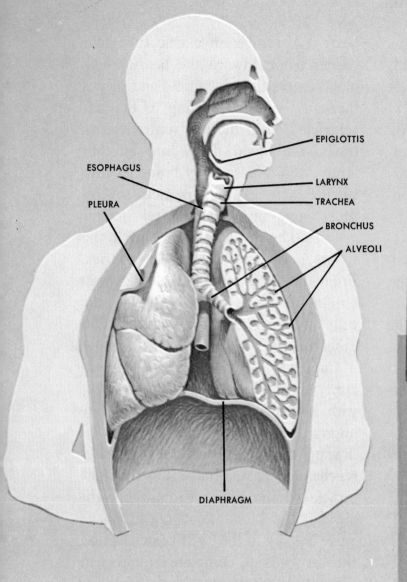

BRONCHIAL TUBES WITH
AIR SACS, OR ALVEOLI

EPIGLOTTIS

ESOPHAGUS

LARYNX

TRACHEA

PLEURA

BRONCHUS

ALVEOLI

DIAPHRAGM

SINGLE AIR SAC, OR ALVEOLUS, CONTAINING CAPILLARIES

1. Respiratory system. 2. Bronchial tubes with alveoli. 3. Alveolus; as per arrows, oxygen enters blood, carbon dioxide passes out. 4. Passage of oxygen and carbon dioxide through body. 5. Expiration (breathing out); lungs contract, ribs move down. 6. Inspiration (breathing in); lungs expand, ribs move up.

The Respiratory System

We have learned that the cells of the body need oxygen, and that the oxygen is obtained from the air. In order to obtain oxygen, we must first get air into our bodies, which we do by inhaling, or breathing in.

Why do we breathe?

Across the body cavity, and below the lungs, is a flat, powerful muscle called the *diaphragm*. When this muscle is moved downward, it causes the ribs to move upward and outward. The result is a partial vacuum that is produced in the lungs. The pressure of the

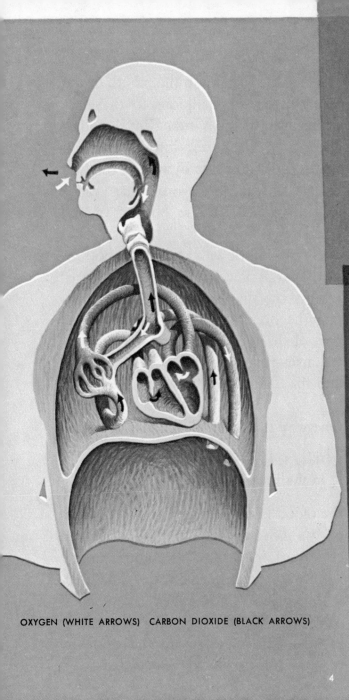

OXYGEN (WHITE ARROWS) CARBON DIOXIDE (BLACK ARROWS)

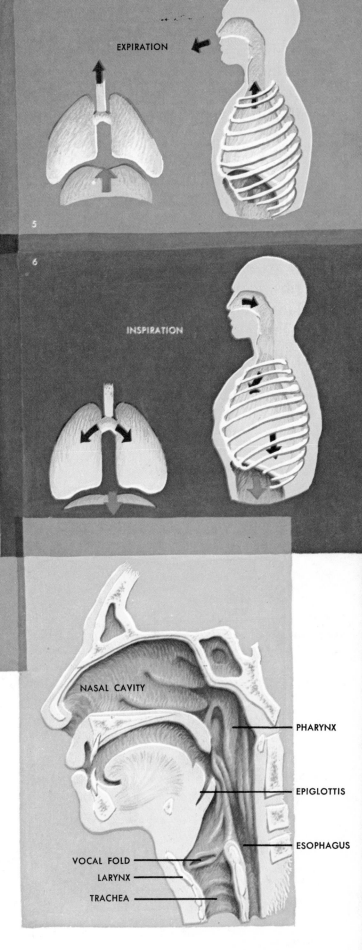

EXPIRATION

INSPIRATION

NASAL CAVITY

PHARYNX

EPIGLOTTIS

ESOPHAGUS

VOCAL FOLD

LARYNX

TRACHEA

To the right is a cross section of the nasal passage.

air outside the body is now greater than the pressure in the lungs, and air is pushed into the nose, down the throat, through a tube called the *trachea,* and finally into the lungs.

The trachea divides into two parts, each entering a lung. Each part is called a *bronchial tube.* Each bronchial tube branches many times until the smallest

41

branches are almost as small as capillaries. These smallest branches are called *alveoli*. The tissues that make up the alveoli contain capillary arteries and veins.

Oxygen passes from the air through the walls of the arteries, and combines with the red blood cells. Carbon dioxide passes through the walls of the veins, and into the air in the lungs.

When the diaphragm relaxes, the ribs move downward, compress the lungs, and force the carbon-dioxide-rich air out of the lungs by the same path through which it entered.

To do this, you must obtain a bell jar,
How can you make a model breathing apparatus? a one-hole rubber stopper that will fit the jar, a glass tube in the shape of a Y, two small balloons and a large thin piece of rubber.

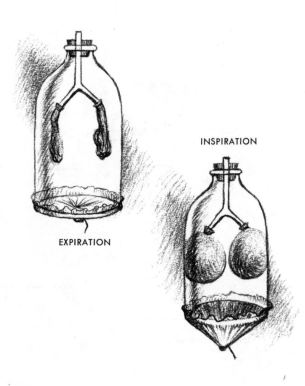

INSPIRATION

EXPIRATION

Place the stopper in the mouth of the jar. Tie the two balloons to the ends of the arms of the Y-tube. Put the other end of the glass tube into the hole in the stopper, doing so by way of the bottom of the bell jar. Tie the large piece of rubber around the bottom of the bell jar.

By pulling downward on the bottom of the large piece of rubber, which represents the diaphragm, you will simulate the breathing process. The upper part of the tube represents the trachea, the arms represent the bronchial tubes, and the balloons represent the lungs.

One way that the cells of the body use
How is air important to the body cells? the nourishment brought to them by the blood is in providing energy for the body's movements. To provide this energy, certain parts of the nourishment stored in the cells must be combined with oxygen. The oxygen is obtained from the air through the breathing process, and is taken to the cells by the red corpuscles.

When you run you use up more energy.
Why do you breathe more deeply when you run? This energy must come from the combination of oxygen with the stored nourishment in the cells. The process of combination must take place on a larger scale than usual. To bring this about you need more oxygen in your blood. By breathing more deeply you get more oxygen in your lungs and, thereby, more oxygen in your blood.

The Excretory System

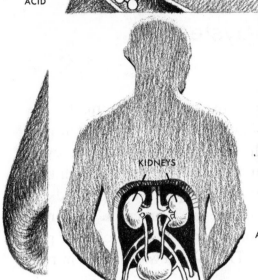

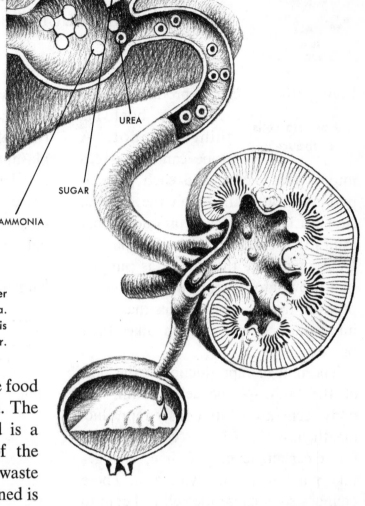

AMINO ACID

VEIN TO HEART

KIDNEYS

UREA

SUGAR

AMMONIA

(Above): Location of kidneys. (Right): Liver converts acids to sugar and ammonia. Ammonia is converted to urea, which is passed through kidneys and bladder.

We have learned that not all of the food we eat is digested. The part not digested is a waste product of the body. Another waste product about which we have learned is the air which contains carbon dioxide.

What does liquid do in the body?

We drink many liquids, some of which provide us with nourishment. Milk is such a liquid. The foods we eat are largely water. The water is quite useful, because, upon entering the bloodstream, it keeps the nourishing food materials dissolved so that they can pass through the membranes of the cells of tissues. It also dissolves waste products within the cells. Somehow, the plasma of the blood, which is partly water, must get rid of the dissolved waste products.

This task is performed by the *kidneys* which are at the lower part of the back, above the hips. Each kidney contains millions of tiny coiled tubes. Blood flows through these tubes and the liquid waste products in the blood are filtered out. These liquid wastes pass from the kidney into a sac where they are temporarily stored. This storage sac is the *bladder*. Every so often, your bladder becomes sufficiently full so as to cause you to want to empty it, a process called *urination*.

How do the kidneys help us?

ASEXUAL
REPRODUCTION

The Reproductive System

Living things can reproduce themselves, but nonliving

How do cells reproduce?

things cannot. A
stone can be broken
into several pieces; and each piece is
permanently smaller than the original
stone. Living things reproduce other
things that closely resemble the parent.
Dogs reproduce themselves as puppies
that grow into dogs. Human beings reproduce themseves as babies that grow
into adult humans much like their.
parents.

The unit of reproduction is the unit
of the body — the cell. Within the
body, cells are continuously reproducing themselves. After a cell has lived
for a certain length of time, changes
take place within its cytoplasm. These
changes soon cause the cell to begin to
narrow at the middle. Eventually, the
narrowing process pinches the cell into
two cells. But the changes in the cytoplasm have made certain that each new
cell has all the parts a cell needs in
order to live and function. The new
cells soon grow to the size of their parent cell. Then the new cells split in two.

Human and animal reproduction begins with single cells.

What is the process of reproduction?

A female animal has
within her body, in
a special sac, cells
called *egg cells.* A male animal pro-

duces in his body certain cells called *sperm cells*.

If a sperm cell comes in contact with an egg cell, the sperm cell is absorbed by the egg cell. This absorption causes the egg cell to begin to reproduce itself by splitting in two. This splitting process goes on until the original egg cell has become thousands of cells.

These thousands of cells form a hollow ball. As reproduction of the cells in the ball continues, one side of the ball caves inward, creating a double-walled hemisphere.

Up until now, the cells in the hemisphere have all seemed to be of the same kind. Now, as the reproduction of cells continues, different types of

Human beings produce children by the process of reproduction. When a sperm cell, the male sex cell, joins with an egg, the female sex cell, the egg becomes fertilized. The fertilized egg develops into billions of cells that form an embryo, which is the name given to a baby during its first few months of development in the mother's body. Later, the developing infant is called a fetus. It takes about nine months for a child to be born. This nine-month period is known as pregnancy or the gestation period.

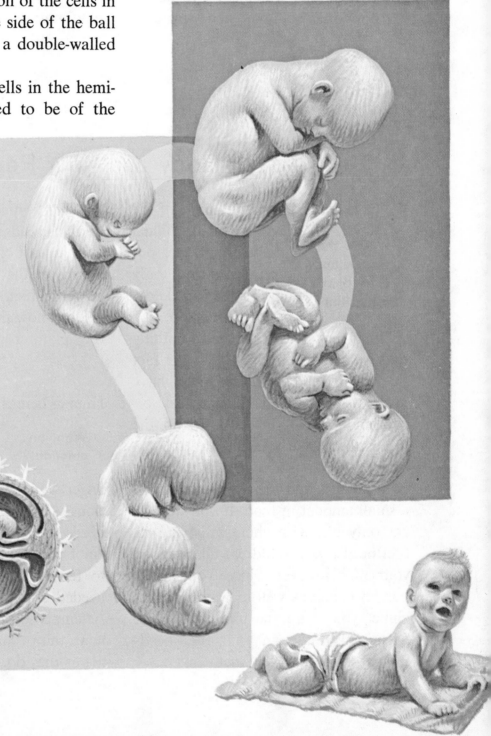

cells form in different parts of the new living thing. In other words, tissues begin to form.

The process of the reproduction of cells in mammals may go on for many months. During this time, what was once a ball of cells begins to form all the parts of the animal's body.

This whole process takes place in the body of the mother animal. The part of her body that holds the newly-forming animal is called the *uterus*. At last, a whole small animal has been formed as the result of continuous cell reproduction. When this time arrives, the muscles of the uterus contract, and the fully-formed little animal is pushed out of the uterus — that is, it is born.

In human beings, the complete process of reproducing a new human being — a baby — takes just a little over nine months.

Your Body and Your Person

We have learned about the parts of the body-machine. When all these parts are put together, we not only have a human body, but also a person.

Why is the human body more than a machine?

What makes us a person is nothing that we can see or touch. It is the fact that we love and want to be loved, have ideas, plan things, daydream, feel sorrow and pity — in short, to do the things that make you human.

Suppose that you and a friend were both hungry, and then you came upon a small amount of food. If you were to act only like a machine satisfying its fuel needs, you would eat all the food yourself. However, since you are a human being, as well as a human machine, you share the food with your friend, even though your fuel needs may not be completely met.

When a machine is fueled, it works until it needs more fuel. The human machine not only does this, but it plans ahead for the time when there will be no more fuel. In other words, human beings know their food will run out, so they plant crops, hunt and fish.

Human beings have *emotions*. It is not easy to say just what an emotion is, but love, hate, sadness, happiness, anger and tenderness are some emotions. All human beings have emotional needs — the need to experience certain emotions. All persons need to be loved, to feel a little bit important, to feel needed and to have new experiences. Attempts to satisfy these needs are the main things that spur human beings to act as they do.

What are emotions?

Care of the Body

Everyone needs some exercise in order
Need for exercise: to keep the muscles in good condition. When we remember how much of the body is made up of muscles, we realize the importance of this conditioning. The object of exercise is to cause the heart to pump a little faster. This forces a little more blood into capillaries in the tissues, and makes certain that every part of the body is being nourished and having its waste products removed. It also causes deeper breathing, thereby emptying out carbon dioxide from sacs in the lungs that are ordinarily not used.

The right amount of exercise gives a feeling of well-being, not fatigue.

Very strenuous exercise or exercising
Need for rest: for too long may produce fatigue. Fatigue is caused by wastes accumulating in the body. When muscles are moving continuously or are under strain, they produce more waste products than the body can immediately rid itself of. When this happens, the body needs rest, in order to catch up on waste removal. Sleep is the best kind of rest and one should get enough sleep every day.

There are many skin diseases, some
Care of the skin: of which are caused by germs. Others are due to substances to which the skin is very sensitive. For example, boils are caused by an infection of certain bacteria commonly found on the

"... All work and no play makes Jack a dull boy ..."

skin. Fungus growths can also cause skin diseases. Dirty, neglected skin can result in infestation by insects, such as lice.

A clean skin will either completely eliminate the possibility of these skin ailments, or will lessen the presence of the things that cause them, to the point where the natural protective functions of the body can handle such threats.

The skin should be thoroughly washed with mild soap at least once a day. If an infection or a fungus growth does take place, a physician should be consulted.

The eyes are probably the most valu-
Care of the eyes: able sense organs. They should not be exposed to very bright sunlight. In the presence of bright sunlight, sunglasses give adequate protection.

One should always have sufficient

light when reading or writing. Rest the eyes occasionally by looking into the distance or by closing them once in a while.

Never rub the eyes with dirty towels or hands. An infection may result.

The eyes should be tested regularly — at least once a year, or more frequently as the case may be — by an eye doctor.

Above all, never try to treat any eye trouble yourself. Always obtain the help of a physician.

Care of the hair and nails: Those who have healthy skin will probably also have healthy hair and nails. Hair can be kept clean only by washing, and a thorough shampoo once a week is usually sufficient. But if the hair is particularly oily, it may have to be washed more often. Brushing the hair frequently stimulates the circulation in the scalp, and also helps to remove dirt, loose hairs and dandruff.

Most dandruff is not a disease. The outer layer of the skin naturally flakes off, and these flakes may cause mild dandruff. However, if the scalp is also very oily and reddened, it may indicate the kind of dandruff that requires the help of a physician.

If the nails dry and split easily, proper food elements in the diet may be lacking. A balanced diet frequently clears up this condition.

Care of the ears: Never poke any hard object into the ear — it may break the eardrum. Glands in the ear secrete a substance called ear wax. The purpose of this secretion is to keep the eardrum pliable. Sometimes these glands secrete too much wax, which blocks up the ear canal and impairs the hearing. If this happens, do not try to remove the wax yourself. Get the help of a doctor.

Keep the ears clean by washing them with soap and water, and use nothing sharper than a finger to wash in the opening of the ear canal.

Care of the teeth: Particles of food left in the mouth after a meal provide nourishment for bacteria. Bacteria secrete a substance which can dissolve the enamel of the teeth, and thereby cause cavities. For this reason, the teeth should be brushed after each meal whenever possible. This will remove the food particles, and prevent the action of the bacteria.

Since it is not always possible to prevent all decay, even by regular brushing of the teeth, a dentist should be consulted two or three times a year.

The hygienic care of the body becomes especially meaningful when we remember that good health is largely dependent on a body which functions properly. Good health to you all!